An Easier Yoke?

AN EASIER YOKE?

A Perspective on Christian Ministry

Trevor Rowe

EPWORTH PRESS

ISBN 0 7162 0476 2

First published 1992
by Epworth Press
1 Central Buildings
Westminster, London SW1H 9NR

Typeset by Intype, London
Printed in Great Britain by
Billing & Sons Ltd, Worcester

CONTENTS

To Lindsay and Alison

who did not always get a proper share of my attention

Preface

There are things I find difficult to do. The greater problem is that of holding many tasks together and finding a balance. Sometimes it has seemed that I have been required to be a juggler, keeping too many balls in the air at the same time. We have all found that to juggle with two balls is easy. Add a third one and it becomes more difficult. Try to manage four balls at the same time and you drop the lot. If we see a work problem in terms of a juggling act then we may be tempted to see an increase in skill as the solution. This is not the way. What is required is to have some principles that determine how we set our priorities or apportion our time. Even more important is it to have an understanding of our purpose that will bring cohesion to our tasks.

What I find equally difficult is to share in keeping communities functioning integrally, with appropriate regard to the needs and ideals of everyone within them. The problems are similar whether they are found in a congregation, a college or a bureaucratic structure, the settings within which my work has placed me. How do we assist such communities to hold together and make balanced responses to the demands placed on them from within and without?

Over the years I have listened to and read things that bear upon this problem. I have not had the chance to detach myself sufficiently to see it with any clarity or begin to understand how it might be tackled. The gift of a 'sabbatical' gave the opportunity and what follows is the result. I am very conscious of its being only an exercise of exploration. I hope it may have a sufficiently open-texture to allow others to weave their own experience and reflections into it and make something useful.

I am greatly in the debt of David F. Clarke, Donald Eadie and Graham Slater who, having read early drafts, made comments and suggestions. A fundamental debt is owed to all those who have formed the laboratories in which I have worked for many years: they provided all the material from which I have been trying to learn. Finally, there are the good people of the Worcester circuit who managed very well without me for three months; theirs was a very special and appreciated gift.

Worcester   Trevor Rowe
Lent 1991

I

Pressures and Purposes

Three clergymen went fishing together on a small lake. When they were some way out from the shore the Roman Catholic priest said he had forgotten his *Breviary* and got out of the boat and walked to the shore. When he returned the Anglican confessed he had not brought his *Alternative Service Book* and went to fetch it. On his return the Methodist minister thought he had better go for a copy of *Hymns and Psalms*. He got out of the boat and promptly sank to the bottom of the lake. When his colleagues had pulled him back into the boat the Anglican said: 'We should have told him where the stepping stones were.' 'Which stepping stones?' the Roman Catholic priest replied.

I have *A Guide to Employee Performance Appraisals* that I picked up somewhere. The employee's performance is charted under certain work characteristics. It gives some examples, and under 'Resourcefulness' marks 'walking on water' as 'far exceeding job requirements'! The difficulty for Christians, including in a special way ordained ministers, is that they feel they cannot set upper limits to what is required of them. They live therefore with a constant sense of failure and accompanying guilt. It is a complex matter, but some of the components of the problem can be set out.

The Authorized Version of Matt. 5.46 translated the command of Jesus as 'Be ye therefore perfect, even as your Father which is in heaven is perfect.' That has scared people ever since. Jesus is seen as setting a standard of required performance, and when we internalize it our attitude is deeply shaped. The text in the New English Bible is 'There must be no limit to your goodness, as your heavenly Father's goodness knows no bounds.' The disciples are not to deny love to their enemies. They are not to love only those who love them. They are to live with openness and this means that perfection is possible, but it is not *demanded*. In many gospel stories we find Jesus very sensitive to the limitations of people, even though saddened by them. Can we be happy to identify with such people? Is it possible to escape from a destructive perfectionism into an open style of holiness? This is a question we must come back to. At the moment I am concerned with how the church, and individual ministers and lay people within it, are impoverished by their attempts to do too much and maybe to do the wrong things. People see themselves required to carry unreasonable burdens and Christian communities are not sensible enough in determining their programmes. When these two things exist side by side we have a recipe for breakdown or at least debilitating low morale.

There is a sickness common to ministers and lay people. On the sixth Sunday before Easter I usually announce that I am giving up guilt for Lent. Like most forms of Lenten fasting one hopes to keep it up for the whole year but recognizes that the weakness is so endemic that a limited abstinence may have to serve as a symbol of where one stands in an ongoing conflict. I hope never to eliminate guilt from my life, for there are occasions when it is wholly proper to feel guilty. What we need to fight is the use of guilt as a motivating force. This is a pervasive disease in the church. The theory is that if you make people feel guilty about something they will take steps to avoid it and submit to your designs. My experience is that it does not work in this way. Guilt is a weak force even though it feels unpleasant. What motivates people strongly is the prospect of something worth achieving. We can be captured by visions and respond to opportunities.

In all voluntary institutions there is need for people to share out tasks. In nineteenth-century Methodism a hugh growth took place because lay responsibility was greatly developed. It was, as far as one can see, not difficult to recruit people for office. They were motivated by their religion, but also by newly dis-

covered social, economic and political aspirations. In secular
life there were 'few wise by any human standard, few powerful
or of noble birth',[1] but in developing Chapel culture they were
given positions of dignity and influence and were able to achieve
through them respect and affirmation. One of my favourite
stories can be read at many levels. The class leader of a Methodist millowner was a worker in the mill. One day he called at
the big house and the door was answered by a maid, also a
Methodist. 'Oh, Mr Smith, you should 'ave come to t'back
door,' she said, for she had a native understanding of the right-
ness of things. 'Nay, lass. It's about t'class.' That was front
door business! Today we are mostly in a very different situation.
In churches, whatever their roots, people do not use office as a
means of seeking affirmation to the same extent, and alternative
motivations are needed. What do we do? We tell sob stories
about how nobody is willing to take on some task. Eventually
someone feels so guilty about refusing it that they yield to the
blackmail. Fortunately not all church life is like that. Nor are all
ministers obsessional. Nevertheless these things are dangerously
capable of setting the tone.

We may deserve to feel guilt, but the gospel surely says that
we do not need to live with it; it can be forgiven and put behind
us. We can then live with thankfulness and joy. We must look
at the possibility of failure to be open to the gifts of the gospel
lying behind the over-busy-ness that damages many ministers
and some lay people. There are lay people who do far too much
for their own and their family's good. They also harm the
Christian community by a readiness to undertake more than
their share of responsibility and so make it less easy for others
to take their proper place in the inter-dependent body that St
Paul saw as most characteristic of the church. Often it would
be better for offices to be left vacant so that recognition of
mutual responsibility could grow. Why must we do so much?

Over the years, and rightly, Christ's disciples have felt that
many of the words of Jesus were directed to them. St Luke
followed the passage in which the call is to 'be like men who
wait for their master's return from a wedding-party'[2] with the
question of Peter: 'Lord, do you intend this parable specially

for us or is it for everyone?' The reply given has been taken to
mean that it was for all disciples. Even the call of Jesus to the
rich young ruler to give up all to be a disciple has been taken
as a bench mark of commitment required of all, even though
all have not responded as literally as St Anthony and St Francis.
All Christians reading the New Testament might well quail
before the responsibilities placed upon them as they follow the
way of discipleship.

However we judge the authenticity of Matt. 28.19, the words
attributed to the risen Christ, 'Go therefore to all nations and
make them my disciples; baptize them in the name of the Father
and the Son and the Holy Spirit, and teach them to observe all
that I have commanded you,' have been taken to place a global
responsibility on his followers. Certainly the Greek Christians,
represented by Stephen, read their gospel obligations in this
way. The risen Christ before the ascension prophesied that the
apostles would 'bear witness for me in Jerusalem, and throughout all Judaea and Samaria, and even in the farthest corners of
the earth'.[3] The story that follows is a sophisticated account,
not only of how that prophecy was fulfilled but of how that
strategy was accepted, begrudgingly by some, hesitatingly by
others, as the proper consequence of the mission of Jesus. The
church has constantly to renew its commitment to that obligation. It has been a strong thread running through its life, even
when not accompanied by very obvious evangelical zeal. There
was a purposefulness in seeking the growth of Christendom in
the Middle Ages that was very different from the style of nineteenth century missionary endeavour. Fortunately there are
always some within a Christian community to remind us of the
fundamental obligation of evangelism, a reminder that doubles
the weight of obligation when we are not at all sure how to set
about it in a constructive way.

A tradition of understanding and belief can exist within a
Christian community and be mediated to a new generation
through repeated stories, its own special language and vocabu-
lary, the undeveloped assumptions of truth constantly uttered,
hymns, prayer and worship. So a deposit of faith is passed on.
Why does the revision of a hymn book or liturgical text cause

so much difficulty? Simply because this deposit is threatened. Not to be able to sing 'Blessed assurance, Jesus is mine' endangers continuity of understanding and belief. When a new church is built a fresh statement is made and there is fear of loss. Being able to recognize the difference between people's obstinacy and their guardianship of tradition is an important pastoral skill. It does not necessarily reside in those who are most sensitive to the changes occurring around the institution that throw into question traditional views and raise issues not yet part of the community's corpus of understanding. The church has not only to pass on the faith; it has to offer new understanding in the light of new ideas.

There are real problems. The fact that four highly influential movements of thought in this century interpret reality in deterministic ways is of some importance for the stability of Christian belief. We cannot ignore Freud, Marx, Durkheim and B. F. Skinner without losing touch with the intellectual culture of our age. These concerns must have their impact upon preaching and teaching. Our greater knowledge of the complexities of the human condition make is less easy to say what we mean by Jesus' perfect humanity. Some who have become accustomed to founding action on the trustworthiness of the world may be disturbed by the notion of 'uncertainty' and find a doctrine of providence not easy to formulate. It is very difficult to know which issue is going to have lasting impact on the mind of our generation. There is a huge and difficult task for those with preaching and teaching responsibilities in the church. It is hard if you feel responsible in some way for the task of speaking intelligently to your culture. Guilt is stimulated if people are under such pressure from other directions that they have to neglect fundamental preparation for preaching and teaching ministries.

At the level of ordained ministry we have seen the dangers and the beginning of an attempt to find a way through the problem. Recently ecumenical theological education has been undertaking a radical review of curricula, prompted by the question 'What ordained ministry does the church require?' In an early draft reply one college included the following:

The days of the omni-competent, one-person-band style of ministry are now over, except perhaps in the expectations of a few congregations and the aspirations of those practitioners of that style of ministry who have not yet had breakdowns.

This somewhat negative response to the question reflects a new orthodoxy that has arisen about what we do not want an ordained minister to be. In 1975 the Methodist Conference required its Division of Ministries to study the pastoral care of ministers. This followed a period of considerable anxiety about the frequency of ministerial breakdowns and coincided with a readiness to look seriously at the health of the ordained ministry. The Division discovered early, in what has been an ongoing programme of study, that ranking high among the destructive factors in the situation were both the unreasonable expectations that put pressure on ministers and the oppressive demands ministers made on themselves. Discussion more widely since 1975 had led to a reasonably wide recognition that both these things need to be changed. Some limited success has been achieved. There are still congregations that expect too much and ministers who keep just this side of a breakdown in their efforts to meet perceived requirements.

May not part of the difficulty lie in belief, or in the problem of belief? I suspect that one of the besetting sins of many ministers, of whom I am one, is not to believe the gospel. Perhaps we have taken to heart the advice of Peter Böhler to John Wesley: 'Preach faith till you have it.' Motivation is a strange creature. We can do things not because we enjoy them but because we fear them and believe that by living close to our fear we shall overcome it. A study has suggested that doctors and clergymen have a greater than average fear of death and perhaps choose their profession in order to bring them close to what they fear.[4] On reflection I find that possibility more credible than when I first heard it. We do things for strange reasons. The motivations of preachers may include, and often do, a conscious sense of God's call to the task (and we need to come back again to this strange notion of 'call') but there may be hidden pressures; they may also be the sort of hysterical people who need attention. There is a bit of theatre in conducting worship and in preaching. Thankfully, somewhat unholy motives can be put to the service of holy things. My wife had forgotten writing early in her school career an essay in which she had stated that she wanted to be either an actress or a missionary. Her shrewd headmistress, who knew much about people, reminded her of it some years later and said: 'You have become a teacher – and you need to be a bit of both!'

Some ministers may indeed have above average difficulty in believing in the grace of God. If this is the case it would not for me be a matter of shame. Such people would not be likely to be glib in speaking of grace. Their struggle to find faith and accept it would show and carry authenticity. Some who do not find it easy to accept their dependence on the gifts of God may get themselves into a sweat of activity to compensate. Much busy-ness can be a way of justifying themselves to themselves, to others and even to God.

In the matter of pressure upon us traditions and their related theological formations do not always help. It is difficult for all of us to follow someone who said 'Foxes have their holes and birds their roosts; but the Son of Man has nowhere to lay his head.'[5] It is easy to excuse one's failures to match the example of Jesus. It is more difficult to belong to an institution whose revered founder said, as John Wesley did 'Leisure and I have now taken leave of one another. I propose to be busy as long as I live.'[6] It was one thing to say that heroically at the age of twenty-four; it was another to live by it until death at the age of eighty-seven. I do not find John Wesley such an attractive figure that I am keen to make him my model; yet he belongs to the tradition I have inherited and his mark is on me. From early days Wesley lived by rule. In his first diary of 1722 he included *A General Rule in all Actions of Life*.[7] More attractive figures than their leader appear among Wesley's early followers, and they made their contribution to a tradition of austerity that continued up to comparatively recent times. When John Lane, one of the early itinerant preachers died after travelling four years, 'all his clothes, linen and woollen, stockings, hat and wig were not sufficient to answer his funeral expenses, which amount to one pound seventeen shillings and three pence. All the money he had was one shilling and four pence.'[8] It is hard to live with this memory. It is even harder when central to one's tradition is a 'doctrine of Christian perfection'. Such a concern for holiness should lead Methodists into a large room. 'Perfect love', Wesley's preferred description, has a spaciousness about it. 'To Wesley perfection is not only perfection of actual acts; it embraces as well the whole disposition which lies behind them, the soul with all its tempers.'[9] It is easily diminished and those who seek it may find themselves confined by the ideal; holiness may be transmuted into legalism. The title 'Methodists' was applied first to an ancient school of physicians and as such should be gladly owned by those who sing:

> All my disease, my every sin
> To Thee, O Jesus, I confess;
> In pardon, Lord, my cure begin,
> And perfect it in holiness.[10]

The trouble with Methodists is that they can become methodical. Far from being devoted to the holiness that can skip and dance, they can become those who tread warily in case the bears get them. They can become obsessional and tidy. It is a sad thing that the Conference has declared its mind in 988 Standing Orders that indicate how things should be done. It is a sign of health that most ministers refer to them only when they must.

Some parts of this austere tradition are fine. My father told me how in his home high standards were required and gladly accepted. He was the first in his family to go to college to train as a teacher and he studied hard to get there, working every night in a cold bedroom, his desk a plank stretched between two beds. Romantic? I thrill with admiration for all that it points to and I recognize how different it was for people of my generation. Fine traditions can however destroy us. Not only may we feel we have to do everything, but we want to do it perfectly.

A sense of individual responsibility has been instilled in us. It is tempting to think that many things lacking in one generation will not be there in the next because better forms of education will have taught them differently. This may well be wishful thinking. I reflect on my own education and recognize how fortunate I was to be able to study both science and arts. Particularly satisfying is it to have had the experience of learning within the camaraderie of a teaching laboratory. If things were going wrong you asked a fellow student to come and look to see what was amiss. You could ask someone to check your results. If you noticed someone else's practice was better than your own you imitated it without any sense that you were cheating. To go from this to study theology was to enter another world. One worked in one's study on one's own. The tutor – pupil relationship supported individualism. The lecturer – student relationship set up a model of learning in which one was dependent on the other. When I came to teach it was not easy to reshape my mind and find a collaborative teaching style based on the seminar. Perhaps things will be different with a new generation. If collaboration has to be grafted onto old stock it may not take very well. The roots of individualism that limit the support we can receive are many. They include intellectual traditions that go back many centuries. They include the influence of 'star' preachers who found acclaim at meetings and services around the country. We live with the relics of this tradition and the isolation it creates.

One of the things that came out strongly from studies of the health of ministers[11] was the burden of responsibility felt by many ministers for the success of the church enterprise. In a report of research given in the *Church Times*[12] 48% of the clergy interviewed attributed the stress upon them to a 'feeling that the failure of the parish was entirely their own responsibility'. This is barbaric in its self-cruelty. It is compounded by a sense of responsibility for keeping the show on the road; it means looking after too much, from the state of souls to the state of the church kitchen. When all that becomes mixed with ambition, of which one is taught to feel ashamed, there is an explosive mixture of high-destructive potential.

Fortunately we tend to be ill with one disease at a time. If it were true that everything we have described was totally and uniformly distributed across the church the situation would be hopeless. It is not so. However, the whole position has not been described fully, not because I have left things out (for I make no claim to completeness), but because there is a whole side of the story yet to be told. It concerns the purposes given to the church and to all those who minister within it, purposes that arise from its God-made character, its missionary nature and the expectations society has of it. To this we must turn.

For example, it is one thing to sweep a road and another to be a Christian minister. This is not to say that one is more important in the eyes of God than the other, but in our eyes there cannot but be a special seriousness about the responsibility that is described as being a servant of Christ. To be responsible to a foreman is one thing; to be responsible to God, almost directly, is another. No wonder some bend under the strain.

I was involved in the selection process of candidates for ordained ministry in the Methodist Church for more than thirty years. During that time I heard a constant succession of similar stories of how people believed themselves to have received a call from God to this form of ministry. It was easy to allow a touch of cynicism to creep in. Were the stories so similar because God acted in this same way within the lives of this group of people, or was it that there was a traditional expectation that God's call would sound like that? After a passionate statement of conviction that God had called them, candidates would some-times be asked: 'But what will you do if you are not rec-ommended for acceptance?' The answer was often 'I shall offer again and again.' I found the touch of spiritual blackmail not easy to handle. But there were good experiences of people coming back, sometimes more than once, and having so grown through their testing that it became quite clear that they were the people God was seeking for this particular office.

It was often said that unless you had a clear sense of call, coming from outside of yourself and requiring you to seek ordination, you would not be able to sustain the demands of ministerial responsibility. I remember that at my own ordination Dr Leslie Weatherhead painted the picture, with his incompar-able skill, of a visit to the Lake District when Helvellyn was clearly to be seen on the first morning and then covered by cloud for the rest of his stay. 'Remember this moment when your call has been confirmed. It will hold you steady when there is no clear vision,' we were told. I understand that. It is good to know on some occasions that one is acting on the basis of an authority that has been given. A memory of God's whispered call does not help so much, because in the moment when you need support everything conspires to make you distrust such experiences. What matters is the objectivity the church has given to the call of God by its decision and action. It is the strong faith of God's people focussed in ordination, faith to which God surely responds, that makes one know one is not acting independently. For nine years, in the preparatory words before an ordination service began, it was my custom to encourage the congregation to respond to the question about the worthiness of the ordinands with a loud acclamation: 'They are worthy.' It seemed inevitable that any sensitive ordinand would be torn by the ambivalence of the situation in such a way as to make him or her open to grace. Clearly they knew that they were not worthy. How could a crowded congregation, who knew so little about them, state they were? To the eye of faith they were worthy, for the truth being stated at that point was that they were made worthy by God's choice of them. I recall the comment of Anders Nygren: 'The man who is loved by God has no value in himself; what gives him value is precisely the fact that God loves him.'[13]

A sense of call may comfort and also cripple by the weight of its divine origin. There is also the relentless pressure of responsibilities. The one thing you can be sure of is that children will fall and cut their knees. The only questions are When? and How often? There are, however, over a period, standard quantities of tears shed! So it is with all people. They die, children are born, illness comes, tragedies occur at rates that are surprisingly stable. Death rates are determined by the age-distribution of the community we are concerned with, but, unless the community is very small or very skew, variations from the norm are not large. This gives a relentless character to the requirements of pastoral care. We do not decide how many funerals, weddings, baptisms are to take place. Ministers know roughly how much time will have to be devoted to such matters in any one year. The responsibility is placed on them by events that have their own proper regularity of occurrence. Alongside responses to critical events in people's lives or the important transition periods there is the chief work of pastoral care, often squeezed by crisis work, of helping people to grow. This requires considerable expenditure in terms of encouragement and counsel. There is never enough time for this.

The agenda for the churches that comes from the ecumenical vision is difficult to assess. When prospects for Anglican-Methodist unity, or a national Covenant, seemed bright (if difficult) there was a readiness to expend energy on these matters. Now it is harder to keep enthusiasm high and justify expenditure of energy and time on these matters beyond a minimal formal level. We are dealing with two sorts of scars. First, there are those who feel they have been let down. They expended much effort and hope that came to nothing and now they have commitment anxiety like that of a rejected suitor. They are reluctant to invest much in work that may offer little return. There comes a point when one's patience becomes thin. Having to give yet again the basic justifications for ecumenical work that one has already given a hundred times is depressing. Surely people have got beyond the elementary questions by now! When we find they have not the heart sinks. Second, we have the scars of those ashamed by failure and who want to do all that is possible to attach an ecumenical label to Christian work. This can easily involve Free Church ministers in a high degree of representative work on ecumenical bodies. They may not begrudge the time involved, for they have real concern for, in particular, their Anglican colleagues and friends caught up in this, but the demands on time and attention are not inconsiderable.

To all these church concerns there has to be added the matter of being involved in the transformation of the world according to a vision of the Kingdom of God! I have lived with delight in, and under pressure from, the bold words of Jürgen Moltmann since first I read them:

Faith, wherever it develops into hope, causes not rest but unrest, not patience but impatience. It does not calm the unquiet heart, but is itself this unquiet heart in man. Those who hope in Christ can no longer put up with reality as it is, but begin to suffer under it, to contradict it. Peace with God means conflict with the world, for the goad of the promised future stabs inexorably into the flesh of every unfulfilled present.[14]

So we are concerned with politics and involved in community activities. We want to give our support to a hundred concerns, use our premises to provide for them, and encourage all Christians to share their time, expertise and money in serving them. The activists in many fields are relentless in pressing obligations upon us and we want to respond positively to them all. I suspect that we are currently endangered by having so many demands that we are tempted to retreat behind barricades. I knew a rich man who was under such pressure to support many causes that he set up a trust to escape personal responsibility. He lived on an annuity and could say to claimants that he had no money to give away: 'You must ask my trustees.' The pressure had been too much; the fuse had blown. A deeply compassionate man had to resort to arms-length charity. The political climate of the eighties has increased the pressure upon people of good will. The feeling I get is that the churches want to be involved in kingdom-work, but many are scared of giving any commitment for fear, and perhaps out of experience, that it will either move rapidly into destructive over-involvement or else lead nowhere.

Before we leave this catalogue of internal and external pressures and try to develop a constructive response to them there is one more point. It concerns the resentment some feel because the quiet centre of their lives, something they long to cherish as fundamental for their health, is diminished. There is a black hole in their spirits; everything is dragged in by its strong gravitational forces and nothing escapes. We know that it should not be like that and we resent it. There should be a free, responsive, gracious centre to our lives and we do not know how to bring it to vitality and sustain it. Traditional obligations to pray do not always help; they seem to be additional demands. Esther de Waal, coming to the end of her splendid exposition of the Benedictine way in *Seeking God*, has shown the comprehensiveness of the call and obligation of St Benedict's Rule, but then says:

> All this would of course be impossible if the initiative and the activity lay with us. Mercifully that is not the case. While we are seeking God he is also seeking us.[15]

This is our hope. The resolution will not be given to us on a plate. It will have to be struggled for, as it is in the monastic life, by attention to detail, careful selection of priorities, and the development of fruitful attitudes. However, we can be held in the process by the conviction that God's will is for us to have joy and not despair.

Necessities and Non-essentials

In the convent of the Incarnation at Avila a manuscript of St John of the Cross is on show. It has a doodle in the margin from the hand of the author. Look at it and you suddenly realize you have seen it before. Salvador Dali must have been there before painting his *Christ of St John of the Cross*; it is a pen and ink sketch of Christ on the Cross looked at from above. One is asked not to look up to the Cross but down from it to the world below. It is possible to see St John as one who set out most clearly an ideal of detachment. 'The Cross . . . is the staff wherewith one may reach one's goal, and whereby the road is greatly lightened and made easy. . . If a man resolves to submit himself to carrying this cross . . . [he] may travel on this road, detached from all things and desiring nothing.'[1] This is not to look down on the world with a detachment that does not care; rather one looks down through the Cross and it all matters but does not need to be grasped at with desire. While held in gaol in Toledo St John wrote *The Spiritual Canticle* and saw Christ in vividly physical terms:

> My Love's the mountain range,
> The valleys each with solitary grove,
> The islands far and strange,
> The streams with sounds that change,
> The whistling of the lovesick winds that rove.[2]

It was the capacity to see all and see it in perspective that made this Spanish mystic a saint. His friend St Teresa of Avila shared his basic outlook but is probably more accessible to most people. She had her visions and ecstasies; but though they are beyond the experience of most there are things about them to which one can relate. In one vision she saw Jesus as a child in the convent. Her ecstasy was once felt as an arrow piercing her heart. Sadly, the image is weakened by too literal an interpretation; her mummified heart is displayed in Alba de Tormes, with a mark on it said to be the healed scar. Her life was filled with prayer and activity. She was familiar with the intricacies of the inner life but also with the drains of the seventeen convents of the disalced Carmelites for which she was responsible. She saw it all as a whole and said 'Martha and Mary must join together in order to show hospitality to the Lord.'[3] Mary may have chosen what is best, but Martha's labour is not to be rejected.[4] What matters is to keep everything together and in perspective.

From this viewpoint we have to find a way of dealing with our responsibilities as we make choices. We decide what it is necessary for us to do and what is not essential. These choices are not final but are required of us at particular points. We may have to move on later to a new set of choices in which things we have neglected have become more important and must now be treated as necessities. Nor are the choices each of us make required of all. One constant joy of belonging to the fellowship of the catholic church is to know that different things all have their place in the total economy of God. It has been good to know when hard pressed that somewhere in some way I am included in the prayers rising from monasteries where the voice of prayer is never silent. To share for a while in such praying communities has fortified that sense of solidarity in difference that belongs to the whole church. About some things there is no choice for the church. They are necessities. The only question is what proportion of time, energy and resources is to be devoted to them. These are things we cannot leave to others.

Worship is one of them. It is a constant puzzle when people say that they see themselves as Christians but do not attend church services very much. In one way there is no puzzle. It is not hard to see that the trappings of Christian worship are not always appealing. I can understand people saying they do not like singing hymns they do not know or unfamiliar tunes. Sermons that are excruciatingly difficult to listen to are preached. There are prayers that are really sermons dressed up in the form of prayer. Some reveal their lack of authenticity when they refer to God, as though he were not present, in words supposedly addressed to God: 'We pray that we may learn, O Lord, the will of God'! The church may be cold, the people unfriendly, the music appalling. Clergymen can be out of touch with reality as we experience it. But worship when our minds, hearts and wills are opened up towards God is vital. If worship is, as Luther believed, primarily the downward movement by which God addresses us, offering his gifts and calling for our response of thanksgiving, then he will find ways of getting into whatever we do, even the worst that we can do. There must be times when we let ourselves be told what we could never tell ourselves, when God reaches into our lives with a new word. This may be when a verse of scripture leaps to our attention and we hear a word of grace or judgment. It may be that a line from a psalm tells us something true about ourselves that we dare not recognize without that prompting. A phrase in an eighteenth-century hymn, or the repeated scriptural phrase of a modern chorus, or the antiphon of a Taizé chant, may get hold of us. I find it difficult to see how Christians can reject the bread and butter of worship unless they are physically or spiritually sick.

What must be the case is that congregations take responsibility for their collective worship. It must reflect their concerns and express their love. This does not mean that many voices must be heard; this can be very distracting and unhelpful. What is done must be capable of being owned by the worshippers. If they do not like parts of it themselves they should be able to see its value for others and how it contributes to the fellowship. The music should be varied and aim at excellence. There are churches with choirs that feel a routine necessity to sing an anthem each week, without knowing what a pain this may be to some in the congregation. It is not an expression of fellowship to maintain a routine that brings no enrichment. Hymns should be chosen so that they use different periods of hymnody and draw from different tribes in the rich family of the church. It is as unhelpful to select only the hymns of Charles Wesley as it is to neglect them. The reading of scripture is of immense importance and must be well done. Sometimes one hears what has been read on a page and transferred to speech without it appearing to have passed through the mind! There are three operations: reading what the scripture says, letting it enter the reader's mind to be heard there, and then speaking what the hearer has heard. I remember a lady after a service being so grateful that she was able to understand a particularly tricky passage in St Paul because it had been read with intelligence. She told me how she had usually been unable to make very much sense of Paul as he was read in church. We have to learn to cultivate what F. D. Maurice called the friendship of books, getting inside what we read to make friends of the authors so they are able to speak to us and through us.

The preacher is not necessarily the best person to lead the prayers of a congregation; different gifts may be needed. Happy are the congregations ready to arouse the Spirit's gift in those who can collect prayer, express it with economy and with that open-weave by which others can insert their own concerns within it. Let there be silence, short periods of silence marking out parts of the service and longer periods that are long enough for people to be able to learn how to use them. Sometimes silence can be guided helpfully, but not at the expense of that hovering almost palpable silence that yields surprises. There is a hint in the New Testament that in those congregations where speaking in tongues was welcomed as the Spirit's gift there developed a cluster of acclamations that allowed folk not so gifted to feel they need not be left out. They could shout their *amen* and *maranatha*, or phrases that sound like liturgical ejaculations such as 'He is Lord of All'.[5] Congregations need a repertoire of versicles and responses, antiphons, choruses that can be taken up to provide vehicles for spontaneity.

Preaching well done is important. 'Well done' does not necessarily imply that all preaching must be bright, popular and interesting. It would be a happy thing if this were true, but it would be a bonus. The important thing is that it should do the job for which it exists. There must be seriousness in dealing with the Bible. To suppose that the Bible is immediately intelligible is to trivialize the cultural gap that yawns between the biblical world and our own. The Bible belongs to different times and places. One of the most important reasons for including the study of Greek in theological education is to help people to recognize through the language that the New Testament writers were not thinking in English as they wrote! It was told of a local preacher in a Methodist circuit on the edge of the north Yorkshire moors that he taught himself Hebrew and Greek so that he could prepare properly for his preaching ministry. We need to get into the biblical world, find its richness and the excitement of its ideas. Seriousness must be given also to the complexity of the human heart and the human zone to which the biblical message must be addressed. The north Yorkshire preacher can stand as an example of the level of preparation that should be aspired to for a preaching ministry. Preparation includes detailed work in preparing a sermon and adequate time being given to it. Perhaps more important is the investment preachers are encouraged to make in an enlargement of their minds and spirits that will make them less inadequate for the task.

Sacraments are given to us to enjoy. Baptism is an occasion for extravagance, reflecting the limitless grace of God. Why are we so niggardly with water? The fact that it plays a key role in the service should be apparent to the person on the back row of the church. Pour water noisily into the font from a large jug. Let the minister cup his or her hand in the water and allow it to stream off, preferably catching the light so that its liveliness is seen. Show off the baby blatantly so that the congregation into whose membership he or she has come may smile and be gladdened by the glory of God's gifts. Preach about baptism not just in order to show its place in the Christian tradition but to stimulate people to live the baptismal life into which they, too, were once initiated.

If we are growing as grateful people the Lord's Supper will be approached with infectious thankfulness. We should take pains to get to know the liturgy so that we can dispense with

books. We must know our lines and not be waiting for the
prompter. Once I attended a catholic mass in Spain and com-
mented to a priest companion about the total absence of books
in the hands of the congregation. He told me that when the
vernacular mass was introduced they spent a few weeks learning
their parts and the show has run for a thousand performances
since! I contrast this with the heap of books sometimes thrust
into my hands at a church door.

There is the matter of pace. Does a dragging pace make for
inappropriate solemnity? Is it that we drag things because we
feel solemnity is required? When things move with not unseemly
haste the zestfulness of thanksgiving is released. Yet the pace
needs to be quiet, not hectic. We need to have time for each
other. It matters that we should be happy to move to Christ's
table at the pace of the elderly or handicapped person in front
of us and enjoy those moments of fellowship. If we are lucky
we may sometimes be able to skip to the communion rail at the
pace of a child. There are customs that shape our responses. If
it is felt that only kneeling to receive communion is acceptable
we lose the marvellous sense, that may be needed at times, of
standing tall to meet with the Christ who treats us as brothers
and sisters, not suppliants. If we hold our hands as a begging
bowl to receive the eucharistic bread, we celebrate in our bodies
our thanksgiving for grace that is there for the asking. If we
take into our hands a chalice (supposing that it is not denied
to us by a nervous minister) we celebrate the confidence of faith
that God's giving has inspired in us. So the sacraments become
important because they are made our own within the fellowship.

Worship belongs to the normal necessities of the Christian's
and church's life. So does evangelism. It is the normality of
evangelism that is important and this is why calls for special
periods of evangelism, made with the best of intentions, seem
somehow not right. Such calls are often felt to be a burden
placed on us. This sense of imposition is fortified if periods are
set apart for preparation for evangelism. In my experience this
preparatory stage can be entered upon with enthusiasm but
burns out before the action starts. The failures of these schemes
in my lifetime have made me resolve that I shall never 'prepare

for' evangelism. Evangelism is to be done, however poorly I may do it. Christ has to be offered for the salvation of all people. There is no doubt that some people are very gifted as evangelists. The writer to the Ephesians recognized this when he said that God has given some to be evangelists.[6] This does not mean that only some are to be so engaged. All the evidence suggests that people come to faith more through the influence of those who would be very surprised to hear themselves called evaneglists. Dr George Hunter asked people in north America how they would describe evangelists. Their replies formed a clear and not very attractive stereotype. Ninety per cent of the adjectives applied were negative and alienating, e.g. aggressive, dogmatic, manipulative, moralistic, arrogant. He also asked people to describe 'the one person most responsible for their involvement with Christ and his church'. The most cited adjectives were 'caring' and 'loving'. The people who made the difference helped them to feel accepted, important or special, loved, wanted or needed. About half of those questioned could not recall anything the influential person had said that made the difference. No doubt they heard something but this was not dominant. What made the difference? 'She was there when I needed her.' 'They invited me to their home.' 'He lent me a book.' 'He helped me laugh again.'[7] All that is needed to be an effective evangelist is well within the competence of every Christian. I know very well a church about which someone said 'It is natural for people to talk about their membership of their church.' At the same church people are noticed, spoken to, encouraged. Not surprisingly people find their way to faith within it. Evangelism is not a burden to carry. It is no ministerial monopoly, though ministers make their contribution to the work. There may be things to be learned and activities fitted into programmes but these should never be seen as necessary preliminaries. What matters is whether people naturally and thankfully want to share their faith, and do so.

All the rest of the church's responsibilities can be seen as tending towards the creation of health. We are in the business of helping people, personally and communally, to grow healthily.

When people responded to his preaching John Wesley saw

them as turning towards God's salvation and away from 'the wrath to come'. It was in the class meetings that the substantial and continuing work of salvation was fostered. It was in that pastoral context that converts grew in spirit, understanding and appreciation of all that God wanted them to do. Pastoral care is not just looking after people, comforting them when they are hurt, supporting them in hard times. It is these things, the acts of care, that speak powerfully of God's supporting grace. Pastoral care needs to be directed primarily to personal growth. This turns the emphasis in the church's pastoral care away from the minister to the church as a whole and particularly towards its group life. It is too simplistic to say counselling is for crises and groups for growth, but it is not wholly wrong. Within a group of people we are able to check our perceptions of how things are as we compare and contrast our private world with that of other people. So our world grows through the process. A group in which care for each member prevails is the best setting for learning from our experiences, for theological education through which our understanding of the faith is enriched, for struggling with complex issues presented by modern life, and for learning with others how to pray. The resources in any group of, say, ten people are considerable but they need support and supplement. It is here that the responsibilities of ministers chiefly lie. They are not there to do this work instead of others but to offer resources as they are required; in particular, to make available more of the Christian tradition than may be available in the group.

It should never be supposed that the church serves the community only when it functions as a collected group of people. All the most substantial pieces of Christian service that I have seen in local communities have been effected through individuals deeply committed to the health of their community. These people did not seek permission to do what they saw was meant by obedience to Christ. The life of the church dispersed in its members is primary; and attempts must be made to incorporate this work into the prayers of the congregation. Very often there are services that can be rendered by collective action, through which the church's resources in property and people are put to some purpose. About the importance of this there is no argument, though too often churches want to be seen doing things and feel guilty if they are not. What is not always clearly recognized is the possibility of partnership arrangements between churches and other helping agencies in the community, arrangements in which public kudos is muted. We may have resources to share, but effective work may only be possible if they are placed in the hands of those who have access to greater expertise.

There will be occasions when our best service to our community will be in terms of prophecy, when we see something wrong or something needing to be done and public attention needs to be drawn to it. Such prophetic ministries only have real credibility if they are based on other serving ministries. There is both a science and art in this engagement with society. It is important that we should draw upon the insights of community development work. Sadly, training in this dimension of service has not been as widely taken up as it should have been.

The 'system' within which we live goes out into national and international affairs and concerns for the environment. It is vital that the church should be aware of the issues and should help its members towards an informed understanding of them. Such concerns will lead us into accepting responsibility for the support of those who do what we cannot do and go where we cannot go. It is here that a congregation has to engage selectively. As a rule of thumb, it seems to me, the church should be supporting the things that do not catch the headlines or command great popular support. It should be careful to continue support when the eyes of the media have turned away. Of course, concern for justice and peace in the world will create conflict. Most subjects in these areas are complex enough for there to be many views of how they arise and how best they can be addressed. Conflict should not be something with which the church finds it hard to deal, though it often does. We know about human fallibility. We know about forces that can drag apart and forces that can build up. If the conflict is with a threatened government or some vested interest, Christians have much experience of such situations and there are resources in our tradition to draw upon.

So far we have been talking about necessities. The necessary features of our common life are all normal. I have wanted to emphasize their normality and to show how our responses to them need not feel burdensome. There remain problems if we are to do what needs to be done with a light, or lighter, heart. The question frequently is to what degree we engage in some necessary work. To that there are no easy answers. Sometimes, however, the question is whether we should engage in it at all. This is where ecumenical covenants become of great importance. The local technical college wanted to set up a chaplaincy service. The suggestion was that each denomination should be involved. The response of the local clergy was to say politely that this belonged to a stage in ecumenism that, for them at least, was passed. One person knowing that he had the general support of all and could fall back on the group for further help as necessary was suggested as chaplain to do the work on behalf of all. I work in a city where an important ministry to tourists is undertaken by the cathedral. There is no point in other churches getting involved separately. The other churches provide people to share the work and enable the one to act on behalf of all. Ecumenical covenants seem increasingly to be the means whereby we advance on the *Lund* principle and 'do not all do what can be done better by one' as an expression of shared missionary commitment.

What is important is not always what you do but what you don't do. This sort of avuncular aphorism points to a truth rather than describes one. Negligence can be unwitting or by design. Because we do not think what we are doing, we neglect things that ought to be done. If we establish no system of priorities we shall be swamped. There must be a cut off-point of things in which we do not engage because we have no adequate resources. There are things that are important to do that are crowded out by things that we should have chosen not to do. One of the delights about becoming middle-aged is recognizing how many things do not need to take up our energy, because we know that we shall never achieve those things that are not as important as once they seemed. Of course the energy released from some foolish obligation may be wasted; but we can plan negligence in order to achieve what is achievable. There are a number of reasons why we fail here. For example, we can continue to hold to fantasies of greater achievements than are realistic. We may be able to recognize our stupidity in still hoping to play cricket in a Test Match when we are in our late forties. There are less prominent goals that are unlikely to be achieved. There are preferments we would like to have when we should be increasingly able to recognize how unsuitable we are for them. I have been in a position to see people spending considerable energy in the hope of particular appointments when they would have done better to devote themselves to more realizable objectives.

Planned negligence requires the capacity to say 'No'. Many people find this very difficult. They live with the hope that they can do everything and the belief that they ought to do everything. Their diaries are filled with appointments to do things. They take on tasks for which they are not fitted. They cannot cope with the reaction of those whose request they refuse. The end product is to regret the situation they have made for themselves, feel annoyed that they allowed themselves to be talked into an impossible situation, and ashamed that they gave in without resistance. Particularly, it is hard to say 'No' to people we feel sorry for and people we care about. How can I, who have been given so much, deny what I can give to someone who clearly needs it? Does not love require total self-giving? So we learn to live under obligation rather than freedom. Love degenerates into a dependent rather than mutual relationship. It is the destruction of freedom that is so demeaning to all concerned. Unless we can say 'No' we cannot really say 'Yes' either. For 'Yes' to be true it must be freely chosen and this requires the real possibility of saying 'No'. It has been suggested that around the age of two, when we are beginning to explore our individuality and the limits of our freedom, the unacceptability of a negative response is pressed on us. It is naughty to say 'I won't!' We are not free to be ourselves. We are owned by parents or by the expectations of others, and become habitually obligated to others. Our perception can then be twisted so that we feel others are similarly obligated to us and we act as though we owned them. As far as planning negligence is concerned, it is the echo of infantile rejection that is significant. If we do not do what people ask of us, will they reject us? But if we avoid rejection by always answering 'Yes', how can adult relationships be established? Can I help a person to hear me say 'No' without my rejecting him or her totally? Sometimes saying 'No' can lead to the discovery that the other does not need me but has within himself or herself the resources that are required. Sometimes the wise person will say 'No' and mean 'Not yet'; it will be an act of trust that the other person has indeed the capacity to grow on his or her own. If I want to say 'Yes' to some things I must seek the freedom to say 'No' to others.

It is sometimes the case, when requests are made, that not all of what is being asked is required. People are opening negotiations! In some cases requests are quite precise: 'Will you speak at a meeting on such-and-such a date?' At other times what is really being sought is the level of support we are prepared to give. 'We have in mind this project and we wondered if you could help us.' In making such requests there are at least two ploys. One is to over-play the demand. More is asked of us than it is expected we shall be able to give. So it is hoped a less arduous commitment can be negotiated and we are saved from the supposed embarrassment of rejecting the request. The second ploy is, to use an angling image, to make a low demand to get us on the hook and before long we have been landed with more than we were prepared for. It is possible to deal with these negotiations in a more straightforward way. We do not need to behave in ways that would be expected in an eastern market, with bid and counter-bid. We come clean. We admit there is a question of personal obligation that may get in the way. 'Can we look at what is possible? I can see what you want, and you need to see what I can and cannot give. Is there a way of my making the contribution I want to give and you getting something but not all that you want?'[8]

Another possibility is that we are being addressed not personally but as representing a network of resources. Some people hesitate to say, in effect, 'We don't want you but we think you may have access to the help we need.' The request can be answered to the satisfaction of all by delegation. To say 'No' for oneself can be linked to the possibility of 'Yes' from someone else. This is not to offer a grudging second-best. It is customary to say that the best person to ask to do something is one who is already busy. I am not sure. Ask a busy person to speak on some subject and there is a good chance they will adapt for the purposes something they have prepared for another occasion. The art is to be looking for the person of ability who has not yet developed a wide reputation! A Council of Churches had invited the Bishop of Southwark to preach at their annual service in 1963. Unfortunately he had to withdraw his acceptance. 'Whom shall we ask in his place?' I suggested his suffragan, Dr John Robinson. 'Oh, he is not well enough known.' The following week *Honest to God* was published! I have not always been able to do as well as that, but I regard it as an important duty to have in mind the likely lads and lasses. The prerequisites for doing this are a positive delight in the gifts of others and a recognition that you are not the best or only person for everything.

It is often the case that we make a symbolic commitment and do not regard it as a second best: it is the best we have to give. People seem to be more ready to receive and value such a commitment than we often imagine. At one church it was expected that I would arrange for the printing of the posters displayed outside the church. I could have delegated this task but decided to keep it as mine. The church was on a busy road and the posters were in full view of people in the buses that stopped at that point. I spent a great part of my time working in the neighbourhood and neglecting things that happened in the church, but I knew that I must not fall down on my poster task. As long as that was properly done it served as a symbol of commitment to the congregation, and that gave me freedom to spend time on others instead of on them. Unless we act through useful symbols we shall never be able to contain wide-ranging responsibilities. To act in this way can serve to reassure us that unlike God we are limited and that the incarnational principle lies deeply at the heart of the church's faith and practice. It is not always a question of doing all or nothing. Being bound by necessity can destroy, as can a sense of failure in not doing what is required. We can give some things a high priority and work hard to do them fully and well. We can deliberately neglect some things as just not possible. We may also find ways of doing things that have significance without them making demands upon us that we cannot meet.

Determining what is necessary and what is non-essential is a thoughtful business. It is a process of management, though we may not have called it by that name. Management is throwing a net over the possible, collecting together all the resources that are available and making them work to a purpose. It is also throwing a net over the future, making happen what we choose to happen. That is good. It is the sin of sloth not to plan our activity in this way. It is also a sin against faith and hope to limit our expectations to those things we plan. We must allow space for the un-planned; we must ride with a loose rein. When the scheme of sabbaticals for Methodist ministers was set up we included one for ministers a few years before their retirement. 'Isn't that extravagant?' we were asked. What benefits will the church gain from it? There were some obvious answers. It would be good to give ministers an experience that could help them see what adjustments they would need to make in order to move into retirement creatively. There was a need to look back, reflect and learn the lessons of many years of often intense service. It would be possible to use part of the time to prepare for the next few years so that the last lap could be well run and not lead to an undignified lurch towards the finishing line. The chief thing, though, is that, like all sabbaticals, it can witness to the possibility of new things. Everything does not need to be as before. God is always making things new. If St Teresa had died before she was forty-seven we might not have heard of her. It was in her later years that she became a mystic, reformer of her Order, and a teacher of the life of prayer. This is a great comfort as the years go by.

Not to expect the unexpected means that we tend to take

ourselves too seriously and make our plans, selections and priorities too rigorously. Determining what is necessary and what may be neglected should be matters of prayer, or we shall get things so buttoned up that we stifle the Spirit. We may not be able to recognize the moment when God moves among us. On the other hand, we cannot pray about our responsibilities and our limitations without treating them seriously.

3

Diversity and Direction

It is clear that a voluntary association functions very differently from an organization in which the active parties are held by some sort of contractual agreement. In a church a disgruntled person may simply leave. In a commercial enterprise they may do so at the cost of their livelihood. The ties that bind the organizations appear to be different. There are similarities. Anyone who has responsibility for managing a work-force knows how much time, care and attention needs to be given to human relations. If changes are being considered it is important to talk with the folk involved. One cannot dismiss people in a fit of pique without exposing oneself to legal difficulties. The quality of work achieved depends to a large measure on the quality of relationship people enjoy at work. In a voluntary association this quality is essential.

In an enterprise that is passing through change there may be times when people become redundant. Good managers will try to fit people whose jobs cease into other tasks needing to be done. This is not always easy or helpful to the best interests of the enterprise. It is better to define the job and look for the right person to fill it. Experience teaches how difficult it is to judge whether we have found the right person, so we dodge the risk and go for the 'devil we know'! This sort of approach is not normally possible in a voluntary association. In churches we have the people who are given to us. To some degree a church has tasks that need to be done and it is possible to look round the membership to find suitable people. Sometimes, though, perhaps more often than we recognize, this does not work because we are following the system of round pegs for round holes suitable for non-voluntary organizations. In voluntary organizations we are given square pegs and need to make the holes square to fit them. It is really a difference of outlook required by the character of the relationships involved. Do we start with the organization as it is and then recruit people for service in it? Or do we start with the people we have and make an organization in which they can serve? Churches tend to work with the former approach.

There is considerable advantage in a large national organization if the structures are similar in its dispersed units. With a mobile society it is convenient for people to know broadly how a local church works, wherever it is. This I recognize but I believe it should not be the last word. It is good to have similarity of structure but there must be sufficient freedom to adapt the organization to the gifts of the people available to it. In fact, to a large degree, we have such freedom if we are prepared to use it.

I think it is important for a minister coming to serve in a church to visit people in their homes as soon as possible. For many of us it is the only way to learn names. We associate them with the personal imprint in the mind that comes from the place where they live. More importantly, it is through this exercise that we hear their stories, learn what they do, have done and can do. Only in this way is one able to see the gifts given to that particular congregation in its members. It is possible to use this knowledge as a card-index, so that when someone is needed for a task we can thumb through it and find a suitable person. It is better, however, to be seeing these people not as wall-flowers waiting to be asked to dance but as people already in the dance. Personnel management is a task of choreography not recruitment. How can this special person serve? That is the important question. It is less helpful, as far as the quality of life in the church's fellowship is concerned, to be saying 'We need this job doing, who is there to do it?' In medium-to-large sized congregations affected by the constant mobility of people it is often only the minister who knows everyone involved. This is one reason why the wide knowledge of gifts held by the minister is such a vital resource. What this should not do is promote the belief that it is the minister's responsibility to call people to particular tasks.

Worship, evangelism, pastoral care and service in the community are responsibilities that rest on the congregation as a whole. So it is with the sharing of tasks. It is not health-giving if the minister is seen as the one who recruits people for tasks. This so easily builds into the fellowship a sense of obligation that is unhelpful. 'We will do it for you, Vicar' is a caricature of sickness in a Christian community. We are not dealing with recruitment but the sort of sharing that is the proper expression of fellowship. So the people to do the asking are those who are already part of the sharing. Others are being invited into it, and a sense of obligation is avoided. Ministers are not always very good at knowing and giving proper value to the pressures on people. If members are inviting others, they are doing so as people who are themselves under pressure. This can lead to an I-am-busier-than-you type of blackmail. More likely it can yield a level look at what is involved.

One very important reason for this approach results from the need of some ministers to make their names by intense activity. Sadly, I have heard the complaint of over-pressed lay people who feel they are abused by constant demands laid on them by their ministers. People look for leadership and will respond to it if they discern its authenticity and believe it to be directed towards the best purposes of the church's mission. But I have heard it said 'It is his show really and we are there to make it happen – and then he will be gone!' The central question, in this as in many things, is 'For whose benefit are we doing this?'

If the work of the church is to be done by a diversity of ministries, attention needs to be given, not just to the use of gifts rather than the demands of tasks, but to the shaping of tasks. To start with, it is good to produce job-descriptions for existing tasks. These should include the listing of precise actions that are expected of the holder. It is not a good thing for people to discover too late that there are expectations they did not know about. The usual things about to whom one is accountable should be set down. Perhaps most of all, and most difficult, an attempt should be made to see the dimensions of the task. This is more than the size of the job. It has to do with potential and scope. When a person can no longer or should no longer do a task, the job-description becomes the starting point for the fellowship to shape itself around the continuing needs expressed in the job-description. Sometimes it will be found that there are things that are no longer necessary: they have continued through inertia. At other times it will be seen that the fellowship has been asking too much of one of its members. Therefore questions must be asked. Is the job too big? If we divided the job would it be possible to take up the gifts of more people? Would it be possible for a couple to do a task together? More importantly, we need to ask 'Is the job worth doing in any case?'

Every institution develops redundant jobs. The classic example is of an artillery drill in which, according to the manual, there was a man who stood throughout it without moving. Why is he there? The answer discovered was that he was there to hold the horse of the officer. The horse had been discharged long ago but the soldier remained. Things like this can happen in voluntary associations. When such redundancy is discovered great care needs to be taken to avoid bruising the people involved who thought they were doing something useful. Rather than get into the position where we are pressing someone to take on a task, the value of which is uncertain, it is better to let the job lie fallow. Let the task justify its necessity by its temporary non-existence and only then see whether someone's gifts should be expressed in it. One manager in industry told how on coming to a new company he found that much energy and time was being given to writing reports the value of which was not clearly obvious. He forbade all report writing for a month and then decided what reports had shown by their absence that they were needed in order to do the job. Such a sensible approach to the life of the church would bring great relief to many.

Most Christian congregations are small, and the complaint is often made that a few people have to carry all the responsibility. I recognize that there is a minimum of responsibilities that must be carried by someone. Someone must have the key to open the chapel door. The important thing is to be realistic about the minimum. We must dispense with additional burdens that are often imposed from outside and arise from expectations that everyone must conform to a particular way of doing things. That every church must have concern for social responsibility is one thing. That every church should have a 'social responsibility secretary' is another! However, the problem remains that limited numbers often require people to go on carrying responsibility for too long because there is no one to take it from them.

When Methodism introduced a 'six year rule' it brought great benefits. Office holders, in normal conditions, were to be elected for six years and could not be re-elected immediately. This meant that an end came to collusion with people who had held on to office for far too long. It meant relief for those who had been imposed on for too long. Thus a much more health-giving attitude was made possible.

Though I am advocating the diversification of responsibility in the church's life, I also want to suggest that we should not just be looking for diversity of operation. There need to be within the fellowship people who do not do obvious jobs. There needs to be space for people who have carried responsibility in the past to move to a rather different ministry: being about in the fellowship as encouragers, people who say 'thank you', people who notice and pray. I welcomed it when a local preacher deliberately requested that he should not preach for three months. He wanted to 'take a sabbatical', to have a break in which to renew his ministry of preaching. One of our sins is that we are greedy towards each other. We ask too much of people. What they give is a gift; we should accept what people offer with gratitude and not make demands or increase their sense of obligation. In fact such an attitude is likely to release more gifts and offer better solutions of the problems we think we have.

It is not very helpful to say that the church is the spare-time interest of Christians though it does point to the primacy of the full-time concern of Christians, which is to witness to the truth and love of God all the time and wherever they are. It is possible for Christians to be so faithful in their service to the Christian community that they neglect this prime responsibility. More likely, they hear many appeals to be witnesses in the world and are not given much idea of what that means. This is the all too familiar emphasis on exhortation rather than teaching. When you are no longer surrounded by others in church but in some place where you are on your own, what has to be done? The answer can be put quite simply, although it needs much teasing out. We have seen that there are some necessities in the life of the church and it is these that must also shape the worldly life of Christians. As the church gathers for worship, so Christians disperse to go on worshipping in public view. As the church offers Christ for the salvation of the world, so the Christian in the world is an evangelist. As the church needs to work for the creation of personal and communal health, so Christians direct their lives in the same way.

There are some silly Christians who seem to feel an obligation to go around the world with smiles on their faces. Christians who learn to worship in church look at the world clearly and thankfully. The daily worship of God puts many more expressions on their faces than a smile. How we see things will determine our total approach to life and this will mean that our witness will be found in the appropriateness of our expression. Thomas Merton used the simple image of a room window as night gathers. When the light coming from outside fades, as we look out it is ourselves and our room we see reflected in the mirror.[1] So much of the world cannot be seen because we do not worship; there is no light from outside. It is our day by day privilege to learn afresh to see and taste and feel the life that inhabits us and all things, and to recognize it as God's gift. It is indeed a learning process and we need help. Robert Browning wrote of how

> . . . we love
> First when we see them painted, things we had passed
> Perhaps a hundred times nor cared to see.[2]

The close attention of an artist can help us. See Dürer's watercolour 'The Hare' and your vision is transformed. At one period I did some sculpture. It was very enjoyable and I produced two passable heads. The chief benefit was that I had to look at the exact three-dimensional form of an ear or a nose. I realized I had never really looked at these features before. I noticed them but had not seen them. A reviewer once wrote: 'To read Patrick White is to move through areas made new and fresh, to see men and women with a sharpened gaze.'

That was a fine tribute to a novelist. We can see the world better through what someone called White's Book of Genesis 'The Tree of Life', or the solitary world inside people through what might be called his Exodus, 'Voss'. There are many who show us what is there. When we see we must be open to worship. We have to take off our shoes and find and see that

> Earth's crammed with heaven
> And every common bush afire with God;[3]

One of the highest responsibilities of Christians is to become by God's grace alive to his light shining in the world. What happens as a result is not their business, which is what T. S. Eliot said about the poet's vision of how things are.[4] When people worship, the world around them is changed. They become glowing witnesses, preferably like Moses, without knowing too much about it themselves.[5]

Worship helps us to see not only what is glorious but what is dark, what is true and what is false, what is good and what is evil. It is in responding to life daily, as we respond in worship, that we bear witness. God save us from carping at the darkness, falsity and evil of the world. That does not help. It does help to react directly to these things and call them by their names. Just as we recognize the pain someone is bearing and it becomes our intercession, so we see that something is wrong and address it. Just as we learn how distorted our love can be when we kneel to receive the sacrament, so we see where deception is taking place and will have none of it. Just as we delight in what ennobles men and women, so we defend the proper dignity of people when it is attacked.

In worship gratitude is established as central to our lives. In the daily worship of ordinary life gratitude is renewed. We live thankfully, confidently and without fear. So often it is fear that destroys our gratitude and confidence. When we experience fear in some sharp form we are able to see how debilitating are our more general fears. One night we had a telephone call telling us that the life of our daughter was threatened. It was a fearful experience that took us over for a time. There was nothing else that could really compete with it for our attention. Our imaginations conjured up all the dreadful possibilities. It could not be brushed off, although in due time the seriousness of the fear diminished. We received with joy the good news of the birth of a grandchild and then a day or two later a report that all was not well. For a day or so we lived without firm information and considerable fear until it was known what the problem was and how it could be dealt with. These deep and not uncommon experiences show us how fear sucks everything into itself. We know that threats set the adrenalin moving. People under threat can make great achievements. What is not given much attention is the burning up of well-being by generalized fears. Of these fear of death is an example.

Perhaps just a little too much has been made of death phobia in recent writing, as though it had been discovered by our generation. This over-emphasis may serve to confirm the deep insecurity about death felt in our society. Apprehension and curiosity seem natural responses to the uncertainty posed by death. We are made apprehensive by its uncertainties. Will we be able to cope when the time comes? What will it be like? It is by definition an experience we know nothing about. This was nicely expressed by Aldous Huxley when, in a *Brains Trust*, he was asked what he would choose for his 'last words'. He said 'I have not done this before.' There was a curiosity there that was appropriate to the occasion! Bereavement brings the acute pain of loss. It also brings the pain of unfamiliar closeness to death, something seen as a fearful thing and normally kept at a tolerable distance.

Christians who worship the God who raised Christ from the dead will not be instantly or totally released from these fears. But the New Testament writers suggest that experience of the risen Christ so changes people's perspective on the world that they can put many previous fears behind them. In the post-resurrection stories in the Gospels we do not find many of the assurances we would like to have. They tell us nothing about what life after death will be for us; there are no pictures of heaven. The best offer is the enigmatic one given in the sentence 'There are many dwelling-places in my Father's house' included by John in Jesus's farewell discourse.[6] What we are offered is release from the grinding destructive form of fear. 'You have nothing to fear,' the angel tells the women at the tomb.[7] Soon there is Jesus saying, 'Do not be afraid'.[8] It is easier said than done. Mark finished his Gospel with the disciples 'afraid', even though the young messenger had told the women at the tomb 'Do not be afraid'.[9] It takes time to assimilate that degree of attitude change. In Luke and John there is great sensitivity to such change. In the story of the two puzzled apostles on the way to Emmaus[10] we see them being helped to find their way into a radically different perspective. The disciples took time to let the promised 'Peace' of the risen Christ[11] overcome their fears. It is a problem needing to be tackled by each person entering the life of faith. In a letter to his mother Luther wrote 'Dear death, dear sin, how is it that you are alive and terrify me? Do you not know that you have been overcome? Do you, death, not know that you are quite dead.'[12] It takes us time to learn this. As our daily worship takes us into the company of the risen Christ we are given permission to put the fear of death behind us and live with hope, not knowing precisely what will happen at death, only that we do not need to fear it. The witness of such a developing conviction is one of the most powerful and needed gifts we can give. By it our own gratitude and confidence prospers.

Christians are evangelists when they are dispersed in the world. The diversified ministry of the church rests at that point only on them. Here there will be sometimes a place for the confident testimony to faith that appeals to others to share in it. Those with such confidence may find no difficulty in the role of evangelist, but many others do. In his Bampton lectures Peter Baelz[13] took seriously the people he described as 'half-believers'.

These are people who do not find they can give whole-hearted consent to orthodox belief: their faith is mixed in with too much doubt. The other thing about them is that they find it impossible to discard their imperfect faith. They inhabit the churches, often guilt-ridden because they cannot show the confident faith that others seem to have and which it seems proper to possess. If they can be released from their shame such people are a large resource for evangelism; they know how so many people feel. Sadly many Christians see just such people as targets of evangelism rather than colleagues in evangelism. A significant proportion of the people whose lives touch our own are half-believers. What they need most from the church, if they are to grow and not remain frozen, are those who understand them and admit to sharing common ground. For such people evangelists will be those who with them are growing in faith, searching, exploring, engaging in the pilgrimage of faith. They may not have all the answers but, like Bunyan's Interpreter, they point the way.

It is health-creating ministry in which dispersed Christians are so constantly involved. The quality of this involvement may well be in direct proportion to their intercessions. Two things seemed to be particularly characteristic of theological students: the fervency of their intercessions and the constancy of their complaints of being separated from 'real life'. In my experience many of them never saw the connection. When you cannot act you can pray. Even more difficult is it to recognize the mutuality between prayer and action. Christians are acting out their prayers day by day. In prayer they have found a way of regarding people and their needs, the world and its needs, with a detachment that then shapes the moments of attachment when responsibilities are carried and opportunities faced. It is because you have learned to pray for justice that you become concerned for and involved in making justice. Because people are made important to you before God you cannot ride over them yourselves or allow others to do so. The working out of this health-creating ministry is different in each person, but its basic method is the same. A great many Christians are very good at all this, yet they do not experience the church affirming their ministry.

Instead they feel hectored into doing things that do not belong to their central responsibilities.

When a bishop is elected Pope he does not cease to be a bishop; he is by definition the Bishop of Rome. When consecrated a bishop, a presbyter does not cease to be a presbyter. When ordained to presbyteral ministry, people do not discard the responsibilities of Christian witness they have carried as lay people. Ordained ministers are required to be worshippers, evangelists and creators of health, simply because they are Christians. It is not, however, the case that all Christians can serve as ordained ministers (clearly they cannot be ordained ministers unless they are specifically ordained). There is always the danger that by diversifying ministry throughout the whole membership of the church we end up devaluing the gift God has given in ordination.

Within Methodism's *Deed of Union* it is stated:

> Christ's Ministers in the Church are Stewards in the household of God and Shepherds of His flock. Some are called and ordained to this sole occupation and have a principal and directing part in these great duties. . .[14]

The Methodist Conference is the final authority in all questions concerning the interpretation of doctrinal statements like this. By its own action the Conference has not restricted 'sole occupation' to mean 'sole paid occupation', for it has permitted ministers to be paid to do many things. In doing so it has stated, in effect, that their sole occupation remains that of being Christ's ministers; it is something that never ceases, whatever you are doing or being paid for. There are other phrases that pose some difficulties. The 'principal and directing part' within the church's ministries needs exposition. It is surely the sort of leadership, described in *The Ministry of the People of God*,[15] that 'releases, encourages and facilitates the putting to good use of the enormous variety of gifts among all God's people in the service of the church'. This is achieved not by being highly directive but by directing: pointing towards what God wills for his people. Methodists speak more easily in terms of leadership than in the more abstract notion of 'authority'.

Ordained ministers lead by directing that part of the church for which they have responsibility towards the purpose for which it exists. Others may do this, but ministers have a responsibility to do it. Their task must be constantly to recall the church to the gospel: to see clearly and understand deeply what it means to be a people created by grace. Ministers offer the church a share in the world-transforming process by which the vision of the kingdom is realized; they point the direction in which it must move. It is possible for ministers acting in this way to be deluded. We are not talking about infallibility in directing. This ministry is set within the context of a community of Christians finding together the truth to live by and the way to follow. In this process ministers have a role that requires them to stand that little bit apart. They must seek a perspective on things deriving from the gospel and its vision of the kingdom, while being deeply involved with the community. Though their judgments are not sacrosanct, they will be taken seriously if such reflective involvement is apparent.

Another area that calls for detached commitment is in helping the church to relate its mission to its context. The world changes with bewildering speed. Assumptions about things that have shaped what was done and is now being done do not remain valid for long. One can think of churches in residential areas that carry on as if nothing has changed, though a good proportion of the nearby homes are now occupied by people of a non-Christian faith. More difficult to notice are the changes in the way people think and the values they give to different things. Ordained ministers touch this context only partially or superficially. The Christian community as a whole is much more in touch. The difficulty is that each member lives in but one area, though he or she may know it deeply. If ministers take care to listen to the world through those deeply involved in different parts of it, they may be able to help the community to understand more comprehensively its context, something not possible for any one of them. It is a high and arduous role to direct people towards a larger vision of the world in which they all minister.

One further responsibility of ordained ministers is to direct the resources of the Christian congregation towards the necessary activities in which it is engaged. This is not a matter of high-handed direction, bossing people about. It is directing people to see how all their separate work holds together. It was a sad circumstance that brought me into a church that had been without, as they said, 'our own minister' for twelve months. The work had gone on so well; people had worked together and great resources of devotion had been released. The congregation had been served during that year by a number of ordained ministers who gave richly of their experience, time and energy. Was I really necessary? It seemed vitally important to hear at that point what people wanted of 'their minister'. I heard many deeply perceptive things. Among them was 'We need someone to hold it all together. We don't want a managing director but we need someone who gives direction.' We are not talking about ministers as organizers. Churches usually have plenty of these! Sometimes ministers foolishly compete to become the best among them. It is more subtle than that. A directing ministry is something that must be prayed for, as Solomon did for 'a heart with skill to listen',[16] the thing most needful but not obviously required. Ministers must pray (and their congregations for them) that they may be able to listen to what is going on without being intrusive and too obvious; to see where things are leading and, as necessary, call for adjustments to the tiller; to have skill to help people see themselves in relation to everyone else with that strong co-operation in which all gifts are valued.

I have lived in the stereotypical village in which everyone knows everyone else's business. They knew too much. People who lived there were in danger of being imprisoned by the past that was still alive in the corporate memory (as Northern Ireland is imprisoned by the way all its history seems to be current affairs). Some discretion and some secrets are preferable ingredients within a community. When all our sins are known, people can be very brutal; but when nobody knows where some of the deeply sensitive spots in a community are there is danger of great unintended damage. The need for a 'confidential person' within a community is not much spoken of, but seems to me very important. There are two sides to it. One is the need sometimes to protect someone when, for example, another speaks without realizing the implications for the sensitivities of the other person. A person may talk lightly about divorce, shoplifting, homosexuality, illiteracy without realizing how deeply personal this is to someone in the group. Ministers, who have proved their trustworthiness, will never be able to protect such vulnerable people from all hurt, but may, because they know what is hidden, be able to take the discussion into creative rather than destructive directions. The other side is the protection of the community from that which is not known and has potential for harm. Again, the nature of confidentiality means that the minister cannot act directly, but usually ways can be found that yield constructive solutions. Maybe this is not central to the ministerial role but when an issue erupts it is vital. A confidential person is needed for community health.

Such a person plays an important role in personal and spiritual health. We need priests. Ministers must show that they are trustworthy and that secrets stay with them. Only then will they be able to exercise the healing role towards which the last paragraph attempted to point. Only then will a ministry to some deeply troubled people be possible. Of course non-ordained people receive the confidences of others. They do so because their reliability is discerned. In the case of the ordained minister it is required, and a breach of trust should be regarded and treated as a serious matter. Certainly such a breach would be a cause for complaint and probably for disciplinary procedures to be applied. During one period of my life my secretary and I were dealing with deeply confidential matters. If at any point she had broken confidence, I should have had to require her to leave. The same level of serious action would have had to apply to me in the same circumstances. It is important that within communities there are people upon whom formal requirements of confidentiality lie. When this is understood, a special world of privileged (in both senses) ministry emerges.

Ordained ministers direct the mind, hearts and spirits of the Christian community by being symbolic, significant or sacramental people. Methodism has found it difficult to speak directly in these terms and has tended to code its high theology of ordination in phrases like 'representative persons' and those in whom 'the calling of the whole church is focussed and represented'.[17] What is being said is that some things cannot be expressed by just anyone. People are needed to say in themselves things about the action of Christ in his church. So 'the eucharist, which sacramentally expresses the whole gospel, is the representative act of the whole church, and it is fitting that the representative person should preside'.[18] The word 'representative' is neither a sharp definition nor a word that carries a width of reference appropriate for rich theological ideas. Words like symbol, sign and sacrament have both characteristics. When we use them we know what we are talking about but, because of their richness, not *all* we are talking about. Theological ideas need these qualities. As a rule I react strongly against the use of the phrase 'That is what it is all about.' I always want to say, and sometimes do, 'Nothing is *all* about anything!' Certainly in our theological statements we are pointing rather than defining, saying what can be said without claiming that all is capable of being said. So we need people who in their own flesh and blood are symbols, signs, sacraments of the presence of the Christ who presides over his supper, of the Christ who is standing by a bedside or in the home of a bereaved family, of the Lord who blesses a marriage or as the conqueror of death comforts at a funeral.

Lay people seem to understand very well the ministerial roles through which people are directed or pointed to the Lord of the Church. Great damage has been done by ordained ministers who spurn them in pursuit of an inappropriate form of egalitarianism in the church. Ministers who carry these roles too self-consciously are not likely to evoke what they recognize they are there to give. When carried seriously, and with a light touch, this 'principal and directing' ministry of the ordained can join the diverse ministries of lay people to form a richness worthy of the Body of Christ.

4

Comprehensiveness and Containment

The stories at the beginning of Genesis are inevitably anthropo-morphic. God is the powerful operator, making everything and moving it around until after six days, when it is all accomplished, he collapses in a heap for a rest. And quite right too! Creation, so vast in its scope, has been reduced to something we can begin to contemplate. We have not been able to leave it there. Too many questions remain. What if, with Augustine, we ask how creation could take place in any period of time (like six days or millions of years) when time itself is a necessary part of creation? How can time be contemplated if there is nothing that can move and so enable us to recognize that time has passed? So did creation take place instantaneously? Did matter and time appear at once? Did creation grow from seeds planted at the beginning of time?[1] Was all there in a latent form when God made it at the beginning of time?

In our century a whole set of new questions has arisen. Did the world begin with a Big Bang? Did most of the fundamental particles come into being within the first second carrying the characteristics that could lead to the development of the universe as we know it? Is it possible or even necessary to say that all began with the creation? That is not a specially new idea; Origen believed in the eternal existence of the world. This belief has now been given a new form in theoretical physics.[2] The exploration of these recent questions is very difficult indeed and we should hesitate to rush to quick conclusions. However, if once it was possible to stand in awe before the glory of creation and believe in a God upon whom it is contingent, it is even more the case now. A slight difference in the charge on an electron would have made a wholly different world. If Pauli's exclusion principle had not been part of the way the world is structured, some of the balances upon which stability in the universe depends would not be there. This and much else increases the wonder. Similarly, a view of God as a creator who embraces randomness (rather than being totally committed to order) has considerable attraction. Indeed the possibilities for richness in a theistic view have never been greater; but, as in all things, great possibilities are accompanied by considerable dangers.

The Judaeo/Christian response to the world has included awe and thankfulness. At best it has been open to exploration. At worst it has led to the condemnation of Copernicus and Galileo on the one hand, and the little-minded rubbishing of Darwin on the other. Perhaps worse than this has been the way God has been made our property. The Bible has indicated a special relationship between humankind and God. This has encouraged us to see everything as though it exists for our benefit. We create man-centred views of the universe to which our friendly God can be attached! We worship the God whom we see as responsible for this vast world. It can be a sort of name dropping exercise in which we boost our self-confidence by believing this mighty one is our acquaintance. We are drawn into the view that this God needs us. What is more, somehow we have to relate all that we do to all that we know of God. So, if I have a special relationship to God, huge demands are made of me. It is great to be lost in wonder, love and praise before him. But what happens when I rise from my knees and on the way out of Church I hear his voice over my shoulder saying 'Now get on with it; measure up to my greatness and this special relationship.'

The situation is not made easier if we accept a moral structure and a moral purpose for the world. If we believe that we know not only what is true but what is best, we are in both a strong and a weak position. We are strong in the sense that our deepest convictions relate us to the one who is at the heart of the universe. We are weak in that we may become cocky (the sureness in our sense of right appears as self-righteousness); or we respond in a hysterical way to excessive demands and become paralysed. If we have indeed a relationship with the God of all the earth we are in important company. If we make too much of it we look ridiculous. If we believe that we should live as servants of this God, that is a treacherous path that can lead us to delusions of grandeur or to life on the treadmills. That we shall consider later.

An epigram that has brought me much comfort used to be offered frequently by Dr James Mathers: 'We are all partly responsible for the whole, and not wholly responsible for the part.' I can only live with the images that have come in recent years from Ethiopia and stay painfully in the mind, if I keep that wisdom before me. It avoids a careless dismissal. I do give my money and my prayers; but I am saved from a crippling frustration because of the little I can in fact do. There are other responsibilities that have to be carried by me; not wholly by me but they are specifically mine. James Mathers did not just give me a convenient escape route.

How Christians look at the world is fundamentally affected by the one man, Jesus of Nazareth. That too can fortify our sense of being involved in comprehensiveness.

Our God contracted to a span,
Incomprehensibly made man[3]

remains the God of all the earth. Augustine in his Christmas sermons loved to draw the contrast between the greatness of the God incarnate in Jesus and the smallness of the infant. 'Embracing all the world, He lay in a manger; a speechless child, He was the Word. He whom the heavens could not contain was born from the womb of a single woman.'[4] Attached in a very fundamental way to the one man Jesus is the whole of the universe and its affairs. This is strongly claimed in New Testament passages that speak of his involvement in the work of creation. The Word who became flesh in Jesus 'was with God at the beginning, and through him all things came to be'.[5] 'In [Christ] everything in heaven and on earth was created . . .

the whole universe has been created through him and for him.'[6]
It is to this man that Christians relate as disciples. It must be
with fear and trembling that we name ourselves Christians.
That is the most audacious piece of name-dropping! The other
side is that this incarnate God walked beside the lake of Galilee
as I have done, died at a spot that I have touched myself. Our
God was indeed contracted! That Jesus ate and cried, laughed
and was weary matters to me. There were moments for Jesus
when he was not running the universe but talking to a woman
by a well, though the man to whom the woman listened had at
his disposal water that would be 'a spring of water welling up
and bringing eternal life'.[7] The incarnation offers us a way of
relating ourselves to a huge back-drop while doing little things.

The Acts of the Apostles, and St Paul's teaching particularly,
depends on the belief that in Jesus Christ a New Age had
dawned. All that Jesus had been was now alive and at work in
the world, witnessed to by the resurrection of Christ and
expressed in those in whom the Holy Spirit lived. This mind-
blowing idea, that God's kingdom was now being shaped in the
world, was seen in people doing the works of the gospel inspired
by the Spirit. It was conceived that a tiny group of men and
women would change the world or at least prepare it for the
changes that God would effect. This experience could have
destroyed them. It was not just some tin-pot business in which
they were engaged. It could have frightened them. The signs of
fear are there in the apocalyptic images that clung to their
visions. They were indeed filled with the Holy Spirit, but not
made into giants who would conquer the world. They became
missionaries who were 'flogged, imprisoned, mobbed; over-
worked, sleepless, starving'.[8]

When God was acting in Jesus of Nazareth, or through the
Holy Spirit in the lives of the apostles, there was involved
the comprehensiveness of his power and purposes, but it was
contained in the limitations of human beings. Somehow we
must find ways of seeing this as a comfortable tension.

In a way it is a good fault that the church is always asking
too much; but there is a difference between silly expectations
and reasonable hopes. Sometimes our targets are based on a

view of the past that is simply not true. Some of the Tractarians of the last century had a romantic vision of how the church had once been. It was possible to select from the early history of the church and the Middle Ages and construct something that existed only in the imagination. Methodists quite easily indulge in their own fantasies. John Wesley was indeed a massive figure and he can stand the fiercest reductionism of a historian. His achievements in the long term have been colossal. What we must not do is suppose that in the age of Wesley all was success, sweetness and light in contrast with present failures, difficulties and dullness. He did not set a match to tinder. His work suffered constant set-backs. People, including many of the preachers, began with him and fell away. There were disputes the harshness of which we have not seen for many a long year. We need also to recognize how much of Wesley's work was taken up, or given a structure enabling it to survive, by others; people like the Moravians, Whitfield and Ingham, Rowland and Harris in Wales, Williams and Cennick in Ireland. If Methodists think of golden days in the nineteenth century when all was expanding and there was prosperity in the chapels, they need to remember also the divisions, conflicts and competition. Look at many a northern town and check the dates when chapels were built. Find the frequency with which one branch of broken Methodism erected a chapel within a few years and a few hundred yards of a chapel belonging to another branch.

There are some places where we seem to catch a glimpse of the church living with a level of success commensurate with the work being God's. In Malta, for example, a very high proportion of the population are still church-going Roman Catholics. Mostly we see the work of God, creator of heaven and earth, exhibited in much more contained forms. The issue is whether we get upset about this. Is it possible to be well motivated towards world-changing action without being disheartened by modest results?

Parents properly want their growing children to be serious, but not over-serious. We want them to study, work hard, take all the opportunities they can, but not so that they are continuously meeting demands. We want to see them play, enjoy friendships, do silly things and be filled with delight in life. The health of the church will be best served if it can live within this sort of tension, serious but not solemn.

Consider some examples. We live with the serious command of Christ: 'Go . . . to all nations and make them my disciples.'[9] That implies, for example, an obligation to engage in the sort of dialogue with people of other faiths that provides the context in which we can witness faithfully to all that we have seen of God in the face of Jesus Christ. To engage in inter-faith dialogue is a good expression of the comprehensiveness of our call. To suppose that we have a receptive audience for our witness (one that is likely to lead to conversion) is to be unrealistic. Nevertheless we engage in the dialogue with realism, obliged to do so by comprehensiveness, but with low 'contained' evangelistic expectations.

Similarly the church must engage in evangelism as though it was possible for everyone addressed by the Christian witness to come to faith. But such activity needs to be tempered by the knowledge that there are features of the spirit of the age that make it very difficult indeed for people to hear and respond. The non-faith character of contemporary society is such that we have to find some common ground before we begin to say anything to which many people can give a hearing. For many the religious dimension to life is so attenuated that to find a starting point is difficult; religious statements make no echoes within them. Do we then give up and settle (as the worst examples of church growth advocacy suggest) for going simply to defined receptive audiences? Surely not. We cannot give up believing that the Christian gospel is comprehensive, but our expectations are contained.

We can look in quite different directions for further examples. In 1969 the Methodist Conference was warned by the Revd Edward Rogers of what he called 'the pollution of the biosphere'.[10] That was a warning flag waved before hardly anyone had noticed what was happening. Now we are all environmentally conscious and different shades of green. There is no doubt about the complexity of the issues involved, although some pundits over-press their good cases by over-simplification. Neither is there any doubt about our responsibility before God for repairing the damage that has been done, some of it by thoughtless greed and some because of ignorance at the time of the damage. We can also believe that God's purpose for the world includes care in building ecological balance, the support of fragile species, and so on. The colossal weight of the problems and demands lies very heavily upon us. We know that for some species it will soon be too late. Not all systems are self-righting. A depleted ozone layer may not be capable of being rectified or its consequences of being avoided. All this lends seriousness to our view of the issues, but none of us can put it all right. Nor is it even likely that politics can be so geared that collective action will do more than restrict the damage of ecological neglect or give total defence against further violation. I comfort myself with two thoughts. One is that in my lifetime the prophets of doom seem very often to be wrong. Happily it seems to be the case that we are less likely to be extinguished by a nuclear holocaust than was prophesied thirty years ago. The threat that came from using aerosols never figured in the calculations of any such prophets. We often get things wrong. It seems likely that we shall go on doing so. The second thought is that the world is constantly changing and that conservation is an unnatural thing. Was it a bad thing that dinosaurs were not conserved? Environmental depravation will contain much sadness but its catastrophic effects are likely to be modified, although we must not bank on it!

The search for justice and peace in the world is fundamental to Christian thinking and missionary obligation. We should be fired by idealism to create a just, peaceful and sustainable future for the earth. In the next week, year, decade, century maybe, we are not going to get it. We may think we can achieve a little of it if we are pessimists or a lot of it if we are optimists, but we shall not see it in the terms required by our kingdom-shaped vision. Are we prepared to live joyfully with that? Can we maintain our idealism alongside realism? Now can the church move towards policies in which we contain comprehensive responsibility?

It is very much easier to do things or work out how to do

things than to decide what needs to be done. Methodists are quite good at organizing themselves into action. Being motivated by the easier option, this ability can lead us to failure in giving attention to difficult policy creation. Policy provides the ground-rules for making decisions about practice. It saves us from being eternally anxious about whether we are doing the right thing. Policy is about making decisions for selective action. It is clear that we cannot do all we would like to do. How can we select areas in which action should take place backed by adequate resources? If this can be done, we may live within the limits of the possible and thus be saved from despair. While being constantly open to new dreams, can we contain comprehensive responsibilities responsibly?

We can determine containment by setting limits to the scope of our work. This is often done without much consideration. We limit the range of concerns we address. It appears to be the case that the house church movement recognized early on that the needs of people were not being met satisfactorily by the mainline churches. People were looking for a particular sort of vitality in worship and for a fellowship characterized by shared personal religious experiences. They narrowed their approach to meet these needs. Charismatic gifts served to reinforce the view that a proper selection of responses had taken place. There is now increasing recognition that the gospel requires many imperatives to be responded to as well as the satisfaction of personal needs. Such churches have taken on board the general evangelical view of personal and world transformation generated at the Lausanne conference. The containment, required at the early stages of development, is being broadened to include responsibilities in community and world affairs, the very things that were on the agendas of the churches from which they separated. The question for the house churches is at what point they restrict the range of their concerns. Other churches limit their scope in various ways.

When faith and culture are closely intertwined, as is the case in many catholic or orthodox countries, the norm of eucharistic worship is satisfactory. A child grows up within a society in which all the values and images cohere with what happens in worship. In such situations Dom Gregory Dix's description of the appropriateness of eucharistic worship applies. 'Was ever another command ("Do this in memory of me") so obeyed? Men have found no better thing than this to do for kings at their crowning or criminals going to the scaffold; for armies in triumph or for a bride and bridegroom in a little country church; for the proclamation of a dogma or for a good crop of wheat. . .'[11] When the culture changes, how does one find a way into faith through worship when the explanatory links have been severed? How does a Russian brought up within post-1917 culture find readmission to faith when its normative expression (the Divine Liturgy) was formed in a different world? In Protestant Europe we have lived with this problem for some time. The Oxford Movement re-established in large parts of the Church of England the eucharist as the normal form of worship. This was reinforced by the Liturgical Movement and promoted by organizations like Parish and People. Today in a high proportion of parish churches the main service for the Lord's people on the Lord's day is parish communion. In many ways this is very good and satisfying. Well ordered, lively, colourful, human occasions are enjoyed by those familiar with such worship. It works well for the *cognoscenti*. What about those who do not so belong? How does one find one's way into faith through the sort of worship that requires some degree of previous understanding to make sense of it? A certain form of corporate spirituality has here determined the scope of the church's activity. There may be an increasing number of Methodists who would like their spirituality to be focussed in a weekly eucharist. So far the policy, however informally made, has settled for variety in worship; the range of ways into worship must be broad. A variety of options may limit acceptability to individuals but broaden it to contain more people.

Churches may recognize their obligation to respond to local social need or issues of world concern, so that effectively the scope of their life is restricted unless the energy and resources are available to carry a broader set of responsibilities. Thus personal needs may be neglected. Those unsatisfied go elsewhere, and the style of the church is reinforced by the ones who remain.

What feels somehow less proper than all these restrictions of scope is when a church creates a cultural environment in which a considerable part of the needs of its members are met in a protected way. The 'chapel culture' that flourished in the heyday of Methodism (and still does in some of its suburban settings) allowed the members to live a reasonably full and satisfying life within the context of the chapel alone. The Wesley Guild movement served and still serves this approach. It was possible within the structured programme of the Guild to be involved in a wide range of spiritual, educational and cultural interests. There was a reduced need to look elsewhere. Here we have a sense of the comprehensiveness of Christian concerns with life together with a sense of an attempt to contain it within the church's fellowship. The danger is that people may be tempted not to engage with other groups in a non-ecclesial setting where cultural and educational needs could be well satisfied on perhaps a richer basis.

The parish concept is based on the deep conviction that the church has responsibilities not only to those who attend its worship but to the human context in which it is set. This is not just an Anglican view. It is shared (in different ways and with similar degrees of achievement and failure) by the majority of churches. One Sunday I attended the main service in the Salvation Army Citadel. The congregation was largely uniformed, a gathered congregation. The Sunday after, in the silence of the Friends' Meeting House, I heard the Salvation Army band returning from an open-air service in which the gospel had been preached in a part of the city that was their parish. One can limit responsibility by creating a geographical parish, an area with a carefully defined boundary or a general area that people recognize as a distinct place. This will be the main focus of interest and work for that particular church. People cannot be organized quite in this way and such churches in residential communities include people from outside who choose to share in their worship for all manner of reasons.

Somewhat different is the town or city-wide church. Here

residence is not primary, as it may be in the village, the suburb, the inner-city or some city centres. It is the church, probably placed in the town or city-centre, that serves the town or city as a whole and maybe surrounding villages. Though they are often embarrassed about it (because it appears to cream off people from parishes and restricts the diocesan region they are supposed to serve), cathedrals often function in this way. Many nonconformist churches do so too. Such churches have a quite different set of options from which to select when they are making their policy. They may choose simply to be concerned with the congregations that gather in them. On the other hand, they may ask what aspects of civic life will not be addressed by the gospel if this group of people does not make them their business.[12]

The World Council of Churches' study *The Missionary Structure of the Congregation* drew attention in the sixties to the *zone humaine* as the proper focus for mission. The concept concerned the overlapping maps that indicate where interests, concerns and activities of people within a congregation are focussed. At one time I lived in north London, worked in the city of Westminster and had tri-national responsibilities. In all that complexity I belonged. My friend and colleague down the road lived in the same community, also worked in central London, but had world-wide responsibilities. What did it mean for us to worship together and with those whose *zone humaine* was quite different and possibly more restricted? Because the difficulty is so great most suburban congregations settle for limiting the scope of interest chiefly to residential life, with its home concerns and neighbourhood responsibilities. Week after week there is (if ever silence is allowed) an unheard torrent of prayer about matters as many and varied as the problems and opportunities faced by members of the congregation throughout the week. These do not find a place in public prayer, because it would be very difficult and would change the assumptions on which many base their attendance at worship. In a city-wide congregation in which residential concerns have of necessity mostly to be filtered out or generalized it may just be possible for worship and service to go some way towards responding to its collective *zone humaine*.[13]

Each one of us lives within a complex system that is extended and multi-layered. When I was at school we used to write our names and addresses on exercise books. Our address began with the house where we lived and went through town, county, country, continent until we came to the earth and universe. Our impact on the system as we move further away from the centre diminishes drastically. So also events at the level of the universe seem to have a very tenuous effect upon us, but at no point can we say that there is no effect. Radiation from outer space may result in the mutation of a cell and lead to my death. Choosing to keep myself fragrant might contribute to global warming. Each member of the church has a life of great extension. At many points there are considerable differences, but fellowship is the openness to others who are parts of my system too. There are layers in the system. I have spiritual, intellectual, cultural, associative and other personal needs that all interact and which may be similar but different from those of others within the worshipping community. The trouble with a system is that if you cut bits out it dies. It lives by its interactions. Clearly there is no way in which all the concerns, needs, responsibilities of, say, one hundred different people can be addressed in any one act of worship. This means that somehow the comprehensive world of a congregation has to be contained without creating remoteness.

God's way of speaking to the world in incarnation suggests how we might do this. Jesus did not go on a world tour. He limited his ministry to a very small area indeed. He did not say all that is to be said about everything. The Gospels must have been selective. John was making a literary rather than a literal point when he closed his Gospel with 'There is much else that Jesus did. If it were all to be recorded in detail, I suppose the world could not hold the books that would be written.'[14] Even if we take only John's Gospel, what the author does is not tell it all. He sets out a whole range of potent images, the exploration of which has led to the creation of large libraries of books. God did not go to all and say it all. He limited himself to one place and a selection of people. He spoke in fecund ideas and images.

Probably the most influential sentence upon the development of my own theology, outside the Bible, came from Augustine. '[The Son] is, as it were, the art of the omnipotent and wise God.'[15] This suggested that God spoke or chose to reveal himself in the way an artist does. It immediately connected with the New Testament statement that Christ 'is the image (eikon) of the invisible God'.[16] It links many other things together too. At one level Christ was flesh and blood and on another he was God for us. You could not separate the two. In a painting there is paint on canvas and yet, fused in it, is some statement. One cannot say where medium and message divide. All art involves ambiguity and therefore its significance is inexhaustible. This is not to say that a minor work of art tells all the truth that can ever be told. An uncertainty principle is involved in artistic speech, and in translation it canot be exhaustively defined. So images have great powers of extension and can reach great depths. If God's speech has this character, there are important implications for the way we speak in our theology. That is a large and very important issue.[17] For our purposes now it is important to recognize that it is not necessary to be exhaustive in order to be comprehensive. Picasso did not have to go on and on painting his *Guernica*. It is a large work but contained. He put on limited canvas a massive vision of our Age of Violence. So the church functions not just by selection but by taking things and allowing them to say something on behalf of many things. God speaks with economy, like an artist. So must we.

Some years ago I visited, during the lunch break at a Synod, a man who had been a most distinguished minister and was now senile. He was being cared for, as well as limitations allowed, in a geriatric ward of a local hospital. It was a deeply painful sight to see him totally confused and being fed ice-cream by a devoted wife in a setting that left much to be desired. I went back into Synod and heard a report on the work of the local Methodist Home for the Aged. If I had not been so angry I might have been thankful for the work being described. The contrast between my recent experience and the picture of a nice home of gentle elderly people was too sharp, and the anger has remained. Many years later I was asked to share in a group that was thinking about directions for development in Methodist Homes for the Aged. We were able to look at the wide range of needs elderly people have and what the future demands for services are likely to be. It was clear that the demands would vastly exceed the capacity of MHA to respond. Should we continue with work that it had been proved we could do well, sheltered housing and residential homes for those who, initially at least, had a good degree of independence and mobility? How could we take on the more exacting claims of the physically and mentally infirm elderly? In the end it was decided to move into this new area in a small way. We would never be able to deal comprehensively with the problem but we had to make some response that also symbolized our commitment to the full range of geriatric care. In 1989 homes at Newport Pagnell and Letchworth were opened. Action that is symbolic may be the only way of containing a comprehensive vision.

Catching up the worship of many and sharing in God's mission for the salvation of the world may need to have a high symbolic content; it may be more effective and powerful because of this, not in spite of it. It may require also a certain playfulness. Churches can be places where, because of our connections with someone as important as God, we take ourselves too seriously. We need in our common life things that have no obvious end-product and the outcome of which is unpredictable. This is how play functions. It denies importance to obsessive activity. A mighty man is put in his place by a golf ball's freedom to go its own way. Play teaches us to be not too firmly committed to achievements. The shake of a dice can land you in gaol or in Mayfair. So we are helped to walk more lightly. Christians and congregations who do not take themselves too seriously and who allow a playfulness to enter their important affairs might serve God's kingdom more effectively.

5

Motives and Morale

People approach with mixed motives that which they may prefer to think of as a vocation. I believe that mixed motivation is natural, good, and may lead to greater honesty and health. It may also enable us to look realistically at the sacralized idea of call, particularly in relation to ordained ministers.

A. H. Maslow's theory of motivation[1] is one of those ideas that we recognize as convincing and wonder why we had not thought of it first. Perhaps this is why it has been very influential. He suggested that we act in order to satisfy needs, needs for food, sex, personal acceptance etc. The subtle point he then made was that these needs are arranged in a hierarchy so that we respond to one set of needs when another group of more pressing needs has been satisfied. So the minister argued well for a better church heating system when he said, 'They will not listen to what I say if all they can hear is that their feet are cold.'

At the base of the hierarchy is the need to survive. Ministers, like everyone else, need to earn their living; but this is the last thing they are supposed to think about. In fact the dependency that insidiously weakens them begins at this point. They are told, implicitly if not explicitly, that they must leave to others the responsibility for their maintenance. When questions of stipend are being discussed it is assumed that they will take no part. It is often said that ministers will not be wealthy, but they will not starve: the church will see to that. What a disabling attitude to promote! What does it do to a family when the one who determines its income seems to be outside it? If they who have a responsibility in providing for their family have no strong position in relationship to this responsibility, then there is a considerable loss of personal dignity. I wonder if John Furz, another of the early Methodist preachers, ever got over the horror of being called from his travels to the bedside of his ill and dying wife to find that under her meagre bed-covering she wore no clothes. 'Her clothes had been sold to procure her necessities in time of affliction. . . So that naked as she came into the world, naked did she return.'[2] That was horrific, not heroic. It was one thing for St Francis to ask to die on the floor, naked, at the church of the Portiuncula outside Assisi. That was the natural consequence of his decision to serve the Lady Poverty. It is something quite different for Mrs Furz's basic needs not to be satisfied and for Methodism to put her husband in the position where he could not do anything about it except by desisting from his apostolic duties.

Clearly the institutional church must provide for the maintenance of its ministry, but a change of attitude is required on all sides. Methodism makes no secret of the stipends paid to its ministers. They are there for all to see; printed each year in the *Minutes of Conference*. I suspect, however, that all but a few in the circuits of Methodism (even many members of the Circuit Meetings) do not know what stipend and allowances are paid. If these are inadequate, it is fundamentally important that these things should be admitted by all involved. Church members need to be in a position to face the question: can I survive happily knowing that my minister must survive on this level of provision? Those who offer as candidates must come to terms at an early stage of selection with whether or not they can survive on the level of stipend that is provided. Later they may grumble from time to time and sometimes get into difficulties; this they will share with the rest of the community, but they will have chosen to live at the standard implied by a known level of provision. The parable of Jesus about those who did not count the cost of building a tower, or get their logistics right before starting a war, is apposite.[3] Sadly I found that among candidates for ordained ministry were those who were wholly unrealistic about their resources to sustain them through the training period. It did not seem propitious for a ministry rooted in reality when they appeared to believe that some angel would arrive to make up for their lack of forethought. One can at least live with dignity, if not prosperity, when one accepts the rate for the job. If this is unacceptable then it seems right to look for alternatives in which one's basic needs are met rather than be diminished by living with a sense of grievance.

Safety needs appear after survival needs are satisfied. In primitive societies these were met by tribal support. They are covered in more sophisticated ways today with emergency services, insurance policies and defence treaties. Are there any particular ways in which some sort of safety need impinges on the lives of ministers and affects their well-being? There may be many, but I name a few. There is need for stability. Where I live and work, where my dependent family is and where my children go to school, where my spouse can find his or her own fulfilment, must not be dependent on the whim of some external authority. I do not think that ministers should suppose that they have a right to remain where they are as long as they wish. There are good reasons for seeing benefit to ministers, their families and the church in some carefully controlled itinerant system. Decisions concerning these matters require, ideally perhaps, that all the parties involved are really participating and that safety needs (in terms of appropriate stability) are understood. This has not always been so in some of the affairs in which I have had an element of responsibility.

Certainly at one time, and possibly more frequently today than we care to admit, problems of ministerial acceptance were solved by a minister being required to move on. This left the church with its problem of the fantasy of an ideal minister unresolved and the minister with a heightened sense of vulnerability due to safety needs not being met. Participation in decisions of this sort is vital, and some of us have had to learn the hard way. There may be good reasons for a move that a minister or congregation must be helped to understand. What must not happen is something that leaves ministers with a sense that they were not involved and that it is just one further stage in a process of being demoralized by dependence.

Every man or woman needs a home as a castle, a place of security. This means that provision of accommodtion both in service and retirement matters. In recent years all the churches have made considerable efforts to bring clergy houses and manses up to proper standards. What I think is not well understood is that ministers and their spouses are not primarily concerned with having homes that meet the general norms of good housing. Of course, it is good if the often neglected areas of kitchens and bathrooms are kept to a reasonable standard. What does matter more is a feeling of neglect, that others allow them to put up with things that are really not acceptable. They then feel, at an important level, vulnerable; and their dependency is increased. Ministers must be allowed to share responsibility with the church for the management of their homes. In my experience such sharing is readily available if ministers are not so dependent on others that they fail to do what any householders would do for the maintenance of their home. Ministers need also to know that there is provision, if needed, on retirement. There have been vast improvements in this area but it remains something to which many uncertainties are attached; there is still a lack of safety and a dependence on others.

One problem of security for ministers is less easy to solve. Their home often feels like invaded territory. They may want to show the qualities of a bishop[4] and be hospitable. But if this role is to have value it must be chosen, not imposed. They need a safe place that is not violated by insensitively timed telephone calls. An answer-phone is only a palliative; the problem has to be resolved by understanding.

What the church offers, to ministers and lay people alike, is a good response to the need for affiliation. One of the finest ministers I have known said to me, 'I could not function without the love and affection of the people among whom I minister.' The tone of his voice expressed a disbelief that there was any other possibility. He was among the most loving and lovable people I have known. We know that it is not always like that. One way or another, the need for affiliation is not satisfyingly met because there is a break in mutuality. My friend loved and had a great openness to the love of others. The pastoral relationship was one of mutuality.

The helping professions are very attractive to those who have great unmet needs for attention and affection. In selection procedures for admittance to such professions it is essential that there be filters so that such people are recognized. They can do great harm by using others to solve the problem of their own unfulfilled needs. However, selection is not always successful. A person, suitable in many other ways, is admitted with this basic defect. We have ministers who can received but not give. Others can give but are unable to receive. Lay people are like that too. Ministers have a duty to minister to people in such a way that they become loving people, happy to flourish within the affection of others. Those they seek to serve must minister to them, surrounding them with love and encouraging them to receive it gladly.

It does not really hurt to show that you are not perfect. Everyone else knows that already! How difficult we find it to admit to the truth, until we try it. Then a whole new world opens up. Not long ago we had a problem in the family. The whole world did not need to know about it, but there was a need for *someone* to know. How good it was to have a few members of the congregation to whom one could say 'We are in difficulties; it is quite hard.' It proved that they had both practical experience to offer and vast encouragement to give. If mutuality is practised a bit, it becomes easier. I suspect that those with whom I work see me as being reasonably efficient, attending to details and getting things right. Sometimes I make trivial mistakes, get a name or date wrong. When someone corrects me I tend to be a bit short with them and then feel a little ashamed (mistakenly perhaps). Being perfect, however, is not about not making trivial mistakes. What I am getting better at is laughing when I make a decent-sized mistake; and these grow increasingly common! For when that happens (the mistake and the laughter) it gives permission to other people to be unashamed of their own fallibility.

We all need status. This does not mean that we all need to be top dog. We need to have a place into which we fit with honour. A distinguished minister I know loves drying crockery because, he says, it is one thing he does well. I understand that. In every church there are people who are good at washing up. I recently opposed a suggestion that a church should buy a dish washer. I did not want us to lose places, such as the kitchen sink, where people could feel good about their status in the fellowship. We must give respect to people and allow them the gestures by which they offer us respect. It does not serve a good theology of ministry, nor is it a very edifying experience, to see ministers pursuing a 'let's all be chums together' approach. This denies to people something they feel important. In general terms it is right that Christians should address other Christians by their Christian names, the names in which they were baptized. However, there are formal occasions when this is inappropriate. Some people have been so shaped by their upbringing that they find it very hard to deviate from the social norm that allows one to use Christian names sometimes, and sometimes not. They feel that their status and (often more important) the status they want to give to someone else is denied by an undifferentiated use of informal address. This may be a trivial example but I think it points to the health-giving aspect of status that is frequently denied.

Status is also given by achievement. Respect goes to those who do things that are deemed worthwhile. It may not be universal respect, for we have different views as to what is worthwhile. It often surprises me how politicians appear to assume that a high place in politics is worthy of great respect. Politics is important, but is not all that important. Respect for the law of the land is symbolized in deference to the judiciary. It was a nuisance sometimes to be living near a Judges' Lodging and be stopped by police motorcyclists to allow the judge's car to pass; but I knew what was being acted out. I feel less happy to be diverted to suit the convenience of a visiting politician. It is parliament, the corporate body, not individual politicians, that merits my respect. Politicians have to earn respect like the rest of us.

Some people do achieve clear and discrete objectives, and I gladly give them the respect that is due. In the majority of cases today achievements are collective. So we do not always applaud the giving of honours when we know that the efforts of others created the achievement that is being honoured. Actors receiving an Oscar often refer in their acceptance speech to those who have helped them. We begin to suspect the genuineness of their modesty, but it is right that we should acknowledge our debts. Individual success has a large element of fantasy in it. For the good of individuals and communities we need to make status less dependent on success. We can be fooled. If a church is crowded, it means it has a good minister; if it is struggling, it is the minister's fault. The status of ministers is related to success. Ministers can live falsely by falling for this one, and so can congregations. We may have a need for status through achievement that cannot properly be met, and so need to be careful about the self-deception that will not prove satisfying. However, it is satisfying to know, and for it to be known, that we have an appropriate place among others in a good concern. This has to do with morale, and we shall come to that shortly.

There are a cluster of issues that also affect motivation at the self-actualization level in Maslow's hierarchy. They are to do with the place of ambition, the importance of self-esteem and a sense of fulfilment in a minister's life. A lot of rubbish is said about ambition. It is a naughty thing, something about which one should be either ashamed or quiet. It is worrying when a blanket is thrown over the idea. When you claim you are not ambitious, it is highly likely that it occupies such a place in your motivation that you are nervous about it. Like most things, when it is taken out and looked at, it becomes less of a threat. It would be good for all ministers to be ambitious. I do not mean those mealy-mouthed versions of ambition such as 'It is good to be rewarded for service by greater scope in which to be of service.' Let aspiring ministers face the issues and find opportunity to talk seriously with those who have done what they are anxious to do. They may find their ambition less attractive. This is quite different from getting rid of ambition by repressing it.

I know a man, a retired engineer, devoted to and an expert in Mahler's music. Not everyone knows this side to him, but he finds great satisfaction in it. I know many people like that. They have self-esteem. It is doubtful whether people really benefit from their skill in games like Trivial Pursuits. Perhaps, because my self-esteem is diminished by my tendency to lose at it, I should not deny to others what they can gain. It may be prejudice on my part to believe that self-esteem comes best by developing an expertise across a comparatively narrow field. Why should not general knowledge be satisfying too? However, for the sake of total health it is important to gain self-esteem by knowing that you have a modest expertise in some field or activity. Sport, music and learning are the most common means.

Self-fulfilment may come best in the combination of routine, ritual and drama that we shall refer to below. It may be that it is also at this level that *call* can re-enter the picture, not at the primary stage when many very ordinary motivations are involved but later when we need to know whether we have been obedient to what we perceived as the call of God. We do not need to attain assurance in order to be justified by faith (a matter of huge contention in Wesley's time), so we do not need to have a sense of having fulfilled the given call, but it does add lustre to a minister's self-regard. If a good degree of honesty has been achieved, it will not drag him or her into pride. It will be a source of gratitude.

Seeing motivation in terms of the satisfaction of needs is a corrective to what could be a burdensome and guilt-ridden idealism. A more matter-of-fact spirituality, one concerned with honest recognition of the things that actually make us function well, may help more. When one has managed things with reasonable success, one may experience a totally different but strongly motivating force like that described in classical expositions of the spiritual life under the term detachment or disinterestedness. It can be seen in the monastic life when a person does not need things but delights in them when they are given. Here it is the absence of need that holds a person in peace. It is a quality of life hardly won; it involves step by step detachment so that the demandingness of life is worn away. What do I need that for? Is it worth the destruction of my peace to go for it? These become important questions. Sometimes, when I face a difficulty, I ask myself what life will look like when it is over; for it will be over. Experience shows that most of the feared aspects of a difficulty do disappear.

Tears may linger at nightfall
but rejoicing comes in the morning.[5]

Similarly, one can ask what life will be like if some felt need is not met, and so come to realize how unreal are some needs and how illusory their benefits.

One of the things that can be learnt on sabbatical leave is the difference between usefulness and necessity. It is good to return to normal duties to find you have been missed but that others have got on quite well without you. They discovered that you were useful but not, at least for a time, necessary. Things go on without us and people manage. An interviewer once asked the chairman of a very large petroleum company what would happen if he and the whole of his board were the victims of an aeroplane crash. He replied 'The company would go on as before, but it would not change direction.' Presumably a new board would have to be appointed to direct the enterprise, but what would be a personal tragedy would not be an ultimate company disaster. It is good for all of us to learn that we are useful but not necessary. So also is it good to learn that we do not need the things we do to make us what we are; we are not simply the product of our activities. It is useful for us to have tasks to do, but in the last analysis we do not need them. Unless this is true, there is no good death. We need to begin early to prepare for that point when we are stirpped of all our activities and are left with what we have become. Finally, we hand back our lives to God.[6]

Some of what I have said about motivation applies both to individuals (lay and ordained) and to communities of people. It seems better to address the question of good motivation for groups of people under the notion of morale.

Morale is a curious factor in institutions; its presence or absence is quite easily recognized. Those who have exercised a peripatetic preaching ministry know that when they preach in a strange church they can tell whether the congregation is used to being interested. I think of one remarkable congregation. When I had climbed into the high pulpit I did not look up for some moments, but when I did I saw a crowd of smiling faces. Clearly they were used to finding worship an enjoyable experience. By the quality of attention a congregation indicates whether it expects something good to hear. These are experiences of congregations with high morale.

Those in leadership roles in many fields have noted the evidences of dis-ease in the groups they work with. Military commanders noticing that the numbers attending sick parades are high will make some enquiries. They will ask the medical officers about the problems and what medical responses the doctors have made, but they will not leave it there. They will ask whether there are other things happening that may be undermining morale. Are the troops bored? Is there some grievance or is some unjustified demand being made on them? One of many glories in the television series M*A*S*H was the way it explored problems behind problems: Colonel Potter was a master in handling questions of morale. What makes a good school? What makes a prison work constructively? Why is it that a particular church is good to attend? Why are some hospitals not very healthy places? It has to do with a sense of purpose, a shared view of what people are there to do. This is the *sine qua non* of high morale, but there are other factors.

R. W. Revans analysed[7] the health records of 600 student nurses who trained at the Royal Infirmary of a northern town. After preliminary training they moved between the main hospital and a number of ancillary hospitals. It was found that while they were at a particular hospital they were more frequently sick and were absent from work longer than in the other hospitals. The liability to sickness was three times greater. They were all motivated by the same ideal whichever hospital they were in. What made the difference? Careful interviews produced one likely factor. There was a difference in attitudes towards trainee nurses. In fraught situations a student nurse could well be confused but did not know how to put the right questions to her confusion.[8] In one hospital (the one where the sickness rate was high), unless they asked direct questions they did not get answers. In the others, the staff knew how to help the young nurses to find ways of understanding their confusion. This meant that they did not need to get off the main line into a siding of sickness. It may seem a little thing to produce such an effect, but that is how it is with questions of morale. In institutions an attitude towards people permeates and determines the tone and health of the body. This is often created by leading figures in the institution. It has long been known:

Like ruler, like ministers;
like sovereign, like subjects;
a king lacking instruction is his people's ruin,
but sound judgment in a prince upholds a city.[9]

Revans put it in more colloquial terms: 'There are no bad soldiers, only bad generals', and 'Fish goes rotten from the head.'

In high morale situations leadership has the capacity to see how things look from the point of view of each member of the working group. Leadership works through good dialogue and consultation. In small churches it is quite easy for everyone to know what is going on. As community size grows particular attention needs to be given to the church's communication system if morale is not to be a casualty. Communication by word remains important but becomes less adequate. There comes the point when paper communication takes on a more important role.

Medium to large churches are finding the photocopier to be indispensable. It can provide short runs of, say, a letter that enables a minister to put church stewards in the picture about something. The whole group can be communicated with through a monthly newsletter and weekly notice sheet, but sections of the congregation that need to know something can be provided with the information by other means. Directories can be issued and kept reasonably up-to-date so that people know where responsibility lies. Reports on committees or working groups can be available not only for their members but for wider distribution. There is always the danger of flooding a church with paper and believing that to be sufficient in itself. It is worth risking over-production rather than starvation in the matter of communication: morale is involved. When morale is low because people do not feel they are in the know, there is a depressed atmosphere.

Alongside good communication a healthy church needs good consultation. It is not enough to be in the know. Whether I feel that my view is considered important determines how I feel about the group of which I am a part. Some discrimination is required in the quantity of consultation. Too many and too glossy communications become counter-productive. It does not help a group if it is consulted about things that it believes can quite adequately be dealt with by an officer or the responsible sub-group. Most church members (there will always be exceptions!) do not want to be consulted whenever someone asks to use church premises. Many of them are concerned with the policy that determines how the premises are used and feel that consultation at this point is important.

There can be difficult situations when a church is divided on some matter. To decide the issue on a narrow majority is not as a rule very satisfactory. Those who form the majority, if they care about those who hold a different view, may be only partially happy with the result. In such a matter long consultation is required, but there comes a point where over-long consultation depresses morale, and a decision has to be made by someone trying to act in the best interests of the whole. The matter having been settled, the church can then try to come together to make it work: the result is a raising of morale.

There is nothing like success to encourage further success. It is one aspect of the power of morale. A flourishing enterprise attracts others. I remember that at one period I fought very hard to keep the membership of a church in a difficult area above a certain figure. It seemed to me that if it fell below that point people would become convinced about the inevitability of decline. An appropriate measure of success gives an air to an institution, raises morale, and provides a productive buoyancy to its life. The take-off points for different enterprises vary. The difference between a depressed and a buoyant village church may be one new family. In another church the turning-point may come when the number of young married couples rises to three or four. In yet another it may be when the wood of three-quarters of the seats cannot be seen on Sunday morning, or when the communion stewards have to think about buying more glasses. Take-off points there will be and they need to be discovered and worked for.

Among the high elements in morale is the expectation the institution as a whole has of its individual members. This is well seen in Theory X and Theory Y developed by Douglas McGregor.[10] These theories developed out of reflection upon the way commercial and industrial enterprises are directed. Their managerial policy and practice are based on certain assumptions. Some assume that (i) the average human being has an inherent dislike of work and will avoid it if he or she can; (ii) people must be coerced, controlled, directed, threatened to get a job done; (iii) people like to be directed and avoid responsibility. This is Theory X, a view of people that sees them possessing little ambition and a great need of security. Others take a different view. They assume that (i) work is as natural as play and rest; (ii) people can exercise self-direction and self-control to serve ends to which they are committed; (iii) getting to your goal is a satisfying reward; (iv) under proper conditions people will not only accept but seek responsibility; (v) the capacity to exercise imagination, ingenuity and creativity in solving problems is widely, not narrowly, distributed in the population; (vi) the intellectual potential of people tends to be under-utilized. This more optimistic view McGregor called Theory Y.

The theories can be written up in terms of churches. For example, there are those who assume that people do not like worship or sermons, tend to be easily bored, only like particular kinds of music, do not want to take responsibility for the management of the church, are devoid of imagination, do not want teaching that makes intellectual demands, have no great staying power and so on. Not surprisingly when such assumptions are made nothing very exciting happens. What about working from

different assumptions? Consider the possibility that people are
as interested in what is true as in what is attractive, that they
like other people to enjoy things that they themselves may not
enjoy very much, that they expect the doors worship can open
will lead into beautiful and good places, that they will give a
reasonable portion of their time and attention to things they
see as worthwhile, that they will stick with things that are
leading somewhere. What if the church works on the basis of
an old song?

> Accentuate the positive.
> Eliminate the negative.
> Latch onto the affirmative.
> Don't mess with Mister In-between.

Finally, among this selected list of pointers towards good
morale, there is good balance. It has been suggested[11] that all
social action can be grouped under the terms Routine, Ritual
and Drama. Routines are the repetitive actions that need to be
done for one reason or another; rituals are also repetitive, but
they involve us more as people and, because they are familiar,
have some stability about them; dramas involve us deeply as
people but are unpredictable: we do not know when they will
happen or what their outcome will be.

It is very much easier to know what produces work-dissatis-
faction than what yields satisfaction. It is so for all activities.
We know that unrelenting routine is not very satisfying. Those
involved in repetitive jobs usually find ways of living at another
dimension alongside the routines. Advertisements for chewing
gum or eating your way through a chocolate bar suggest this.
We also know that we could not cope if all our life was filled
with drama: it would be too exhausting. What tends to produce
a satisfying regime is a judicious mixture of all these factors.
Ritual is often neglected and not recognized as important. We
often use it to build a bridge that joins routine and drama. In
various ways we try to keep a due proportion of these things
in our daily lives. 'All work and no play makes Jack a dull boy.'
This applies if the work is largely routine and play provides the

balancing drama of sport or the balancing rituals of pigeon breeding. Some of the jobs that have tended to carry high levels of job-satisfaction combine these things. A hospital consultant leading a procession round the beds, stretching back from himself to the student nurse, was a rather pompous display. But it provided a high-profile ritual, much diminished in modern practice, that combined with many routines and the occasional drama of a cardiac arrest to provide a nurse with a sense of worth at many levels. Sadly it is often the case that, when changes take place, these elements in the total *milieu* are not attended to.

The balance between routine, ritual and drama is often there in the life of a minister, and attention given to it when things are felt to be wrong might yield a good dividend. Institutions need also to reflect on how they are made healthy if they attend to the degrees of routine, ritual and drama to be found in their activities. Have they got the balance right?

6

Accountability and Appraisal

When the already well advanced counselling movement in this country was going overboard for the non-directive approach, Dr R. A. Lambourne published an important article, *Authority and Acceptance in Pastoral Counselling*.[1] He was concerned to show that in the Bible the action of God is seen in terms of acceptance and wrath. God does not always stand alongside his children but sometimes confronts them. 'The God made known to us in the Bible is one whose love maintains in creative activity both confrontation and acceptance, wrath and promise.' What is more, the person who aims to bring health to others must be seen by them as an open, accepting figure and also, in appropriate circumstances, one who challenges and sometimes condemns. Since God combines these functions, health is stimulated by not separating them. The complementary nature of the functions needs to be seen.

It was certainly right that pastoral relationships in this country should be challenged by Carl Rogers, the classic exponent of non-directive counselling.[2] Ministers had too often, and too long, been seen by others and by themselves as advice givers. Ministry was listening to problems and then telling people how to handle them. Rogers showed how great were the resources of people to deal with their own problems if they could be supported in doing so. What many people needed was someone to whom they could speak openly and fearlessly, expecting no accusation or high and mighty advice. They looked for someone to help them to see to the heart of their need and to find resources to meet it. There is no doubt about the appropriateness of such an approach for most people in most situations. Bob Lambourne was right, however, to draw attention to those times when, in order to find health, people needed challenge and restrained direction.[3]

Grace and gratitude, as we shall see in the next chapter, are fundamental but not all that Christian faith can offer. There is what feels to be a sharper side to the action of God for our wholeness. As with counselling and with Christian attitudes to judgment generally, it was important to correct hard and cold approaches to the holiness of God. The response of most people to the homily on Hell in James Joyce's *Portrait of the Artist as a Young Man*, or to the paintings of Hieronymous Bosch, indicates that over-blown descriptions of God's disapproval bear little fruit. We can be transfixed by that which threatens, as by a cobra ready to strike; or we simply dismiss it as lacking credibility. In reaction Christian preachers have tended to project an over-benevolent view of God, one who would not dream of condemning his children. He might be cross with them for their foolishness but not much more. It is to the *Dream of Gerontius* (that special blend of two different art forms: the poetry of Newman and the music of Elgar) that I frequently turn for a different perspective. For all the thrill of the blaze, as Elgar called it, when the heavenly choir sings 'Praise to the Holiest in the height', it is not, for me, the high point of the drama. That is in the cry of Gerontius that follows:

Take me away, and in the lowest deep
There let me be,
And there in hope the lone night-watches keep,
Told out for me.

And so we are led into a most convincing statement of the need for purgatory. We are prepared for it earlier in the conversation between the Angel and Gerontius.

. . . shall I see
My dearest Master, when I reach His throne?

Gerontius asks. And the Angel replies:

> . . . that sight of the Most Fair
> Will gladden thee, but it will pierce thee too.

Then he is told of the one (clearly a reference to the receiving of the stigmata by St Francis) who

> Was given communion with the Crucified –
> Such that the Master's very wounds were stamped
> Upon his flesh . . .
> Learn that the flame of the Everlasting Love
> Doth burn ere it transform.

It is with such painful comfort that Gerontius lets himself be lowered into the cleansing stream until he is ready to

> . . . rise, and go above,
> And see [God] in the truth of everlasting day.

Blessing and judgment, affirmation and correction, love and wrath, belong together. Accountability and appraisal can be the means whereby at best we increase in holiness, and at worst get in some exercise for the Day of Judgment!

If life is indeed a free gift from God, then the freeness of it appears to be conditioned if he stands in judgment on its use. We know how demeaning it is for strings to be attached to generosity. 'I shall give you this, but here is what you must do with it.' There is good instinct in objecting to paternalism. On the other hand, we feel that freedom without responsibility is also unacceptable. Whenever the free grace of God is emphasized there is the danger of antinomianism. The free gift of God may encourage us to believe that in his economy there are no laws. Both Luther and Wesley struggled with this practical as well as theological problem. The resolution of it has been found by disciples who respond to grace with gratitude. The love of God awakens a readiness to respond with responsibility. If this is how God treats me, then I must live in ways that honour him and fulfil his purposes for me. If accountability is demanded, the response is likely to be grudging. If it is an expression of our responsibility to God that is freely and gladly given, then it will be creative.

To whom are we responsible? Is it to God, ourselves, authorities, the people with whom we work, families and friends? In different ways it is to all of these. The important thing is to recognize the different characteristics of accountability we have in different relationships. Informal and formal accountability are different and must be treated in different ways. Some requirements of accountability placed on us may need to be denied. This is usually the case when people feel they must guard their professional independence. It is necessary also to see that what we feel about accountability is as important as the account we are required to make.

The great way (often used) of avoiding honest accountability is to say that we are responsible only to God. In the end it is true, but I distrust those who say it. I suspect that it means 'I am going to keep everyone at a distance and have my own ways of handling God!' If we do not learn to be accountable to each other in appropriate ways, we are not likely to be very good at accountability towards God and ourselves. When the fourth Lateran Council gave formal encouragement to the development of a penitential system it was responding to the power of human self-deception. It is one thing to leave penitence to occasional moments and to the perils of a conscience trained to be quiescent. It is another to set it within the context of an act the completion of which depends upon a priest believing that the act has been sincere and complete. There are failures that we will not treat seriously even in our prayers. It is only when we have to name them in some human relationship that they can be dealt with. We are indeed answerable to God and this must be a dimension of our living. In Picasso's great picture *Guernica* we have a powerful statement of the brutality and pain in our age of violence. At the top centre, shining coldly on the scene, is an electric light where the eye of God might be in an older iconography. The artist sees no benevolent observer of the world. How different was the view of Luther, who saw all life lived before God (*coram Deo*) and bathed in the warmth of his grace. The righteousness which is imputed to us by faith must be realized in us. Living each moment before God is how the working of God's grace proceeds.

At one stage I was involved in controversy with the establishment of the Methodist Church. Two of us thought that an injustice was being done. We were assured that the church's constitution had not been violated; and there was pressure upon us to keep quiet and leave things alone. At a critical point in the dispute my friend said 'But I have to look at myself each day in the shaving mirror. We cannot give up now.' We did not; and eventually a change in the constitution was secured. We are accountable to ourselves. This must be treated with great seriousness by ministers who have a pretty free hand about how they spend their time and how much time they spend. Not many have any real temptation to steal from the petty cash. There may be some who are careless in money matters, but few are dishonest. It is not so easy for them to monitor what counts for a good day's work. Most of them grossly exceed what is required, so denying the people they serve a fresh and cheerful spirit, and cheating their families of their proper due. It is possible, however, to waste time. We use it on things that have no substance, but they keep us busy and give a reason for avoiding other more weighty matters in which we are reluctant to involve ourselves. As with our sense of responsibility to God, so our responsibility to ourselves is in danger of being shaped by our fears and failures. On our own we do not see things clearly. The entrance of others into the picture helps us greatly.

As in other churches, there are formal structures of accountability in the Methodist Church. Certainly all Methodists are subject to discipline. If members or ministers commit an act that is 'incompatible with the office held or the standing of the person involved in relation to the church', a charge can be brought against them. There are clearly defined procedures in which great care is taken to preserve the rights of natural justice and of opportunity for appeal. In the end a minister may cease to be 'in connexion' with the Methodist Conference (i.e., be expelled), or a local preacher may be 'taken off the Plan' so

that he or she no longer preaches, or a member may cease to
be such. In matters of grave concern the Methodist Church has
very real formal accountability built into its fellowship. Each
year the membership roll of every church has to be considered
by its pastoral committee and recommendations made to the
Church Council. If members have ceased to be part of the
fellowship or to avail themselves of 'the means of grace', there
are procedures for their names to be removed. Each year enquiries are made at the Circuit Local Preachers' Meeting about the
worthiness of the preachers to continue their preaching ministry.
At the Ministerial Synod of each District ordained ministers are
required to reaffirm that they 'continue faithfully to discharge
the obligations laid upon [them] by the ministry which [they]
have received from the Lord Jesus . . . [and] continue to believe
and preach our doctrines and observe and administer our discipline'. Clearly there is much in this that is merely formal. Like
many formal matters they are usually there to be reminders of
the more important matters to which they point.

Sometimes things go wrong that would not warrant a 'charge'
being brought against someone. Perhaps the word 'complaint'
indicates the right level. If someone really falls down in their
responsibility to the rest of us, something needs to be done
about it. I can think of a number of occasions when it would
have been justified for people to complain at things I did. There
is, of course, the sort of complaining that can be all too frequent
in an intimate community. Thomas Merton spoke from his
experience as a monk about the occasions when some brother
would 'proclaim' another in chapter for some minor fault. The
Rule of St Benedict (the basis of the common life of the Cisterci-
ans) provided for such complaints. It had to do so if there was
to be obedience to Christ's command to bring disputes to the
fellowship.[4] When trivial matters are raised in this way the
Rule is abused and serves the scrupulosity or bad temper of an
individual more than it serves the community. In Methodism
there is a semi-formal expectation that any complaint of a
reasonably serious, but not heinous, nature would be referred
to and dealt with by the Superintendent minister of the circuit.
The United Methodist Church of America has had to make

arrangements for complaints of sexual harassment to be heard. How would such matters be dealt with here? I should expect the Superintendent to deal with them. What if he or she were involved or was not prepared to treat them seriously? The Chairman of the District could be called to help on an informal basis but not on a formal basis unless the Superintendent invited him to do so. There are restrictions on the entry of a Chairman into the affairs of a circuit.[5] What is not widely known is that these restrictions can be over-ridden by the President of the Conference,[6] who can agree to a request for an enquiry to be made. The President can appoint anyone (including the Chairman of the District) to make an enquiry and report on his or her behalf. It is then for the President to decide what action should be taken on behalf of the Conference. Fortunately the arrangements pertaining to formal accountability in the matter of charges or complaints rarely need to be used. It is important that they are there.

Ministers are not formally accountable to the churches for which they are pastorally responsible. The only point where, in the normal run of events, a Methodist church can register the fact that it has such accountability is when consideration has to be given to whether the period of service of a minister in a circuit should be extended. The circuit stewards will convene a meeting at which representatives of the church stewards will consider the minister's 'work and influence in the churches and the community'. They then bring a report to the Circuit General Purposes Committee. The sad thing is that very often this is the first occasion when the question of accountability has been seriously considered. Up to that point it may have been simply a matter of gossip. How much better it would be if there were instituted informal arrangements where questions of mutual accountability in a congregation could be worked at on a regular basis. We must consider this further under the subject of appraisal. Whether there are developments in this area or not, an informal sense of mutual responsibility can be established within a church. In this way ministers would not be, at least in general terms, in doubt about the opinions of others because, as an expression of fellowship, they would be told. Similarly ministers would make clear, though not in a badgering way, what they expect of members of the congregation.

If the informal levels of mutual accountability are right, the need for formal arrangements may be less vital. When informality does not lead to mutual understanding, formal arrangements may help, but the greatest benefits come through the development of simple trust.

In an exercise that resulted in a report, *Uncomfortable Chairs*, that I wrote on behalf of the Division of Ministries of the Methodist Church we enquired of District Chairmen, College Tutors and Divisional Secretaries not only to whom they were formally accountable, but to whom they felt accountable. In general terms College Tutors and Divisional Secretaries felt accountable to those to whom they were formally accountable. District Chairmen were less clear about their formal accountability. Not surprisingly they had a wider range of suggestions of those to whom they felt accountable. The impression gained was that poor formal structures lead to high levels of anxiety in this matter. That was an expected result, but it was useful to have it confirmed. One will never be free from some anxiety when one is accountable to Uncle Tom Cobley and all, but such anxiety can be contained if there are points where formal accountability can be registered.

Most discussions of the procedures in the realm of accountability have to be prefaced by a semantic discussion. No word seems quite adequate.[7] The best of imperfect words seems to be 'appraisal' and this I shall use.

What seems to me to be basic is that no appraisal of any one person should take place unless it is seen in relation to the work of the whole Christian congregation. If we are to treat with seriousness the phrase 'the Ministry of the whole People of God', or consider St Paul's image of the Body of Christ properly, then we cannot single out for separate treatment one part of that ministry or one member of that body. It may be necessary, as I think it is, to appraise those who have a 'principal and directing part' within the whole, but only if questions of mutual responsibility and accountability are given their proper place. Grumbling always tends to be uni-directional. We are absolved from responsibility in our grumbles. The same is true of gossip. Grumbling and gossip do no good in any community because, in the first place, they deal with only part of the whole and, in the second place, they increase pride by setting people over against those about whom they complain. It may indeed be the case that preachers can be helped to be more interesting. They are not likely to be helped by the grumbles that fortify the expectation of boredom and form a heightened obstacle over which preachers have to reach in order to command interest. There must be better ways. When I criticize negatively I take on an obligation to carry my proper responsibility for part of what is condemned and for doing all in my power to correct it. When this is not so, I fall into sin.

It is of crucial importance to see from the beginning that appraisal is not a process of ferreting about for negative criticism. First and foremost it is about affirmation. We tend not to be very good at that, and then wonder why people do not flourish. Nearly thirty years ago I was involved in the assessment of a young minister's readiness for ordination. The report of his Superintendent minister was very negative; there were many complaints and there was something worrying about their character. I asked, 'What responsibility is this man really given?' That unlocked the door. We found that he was kept in his place, not trusted very much, not allowed to take a lead and so on. 'How do you expect him to grow if you do not affirm the latent ability that was perceived in him when he was accepted as a candidate for the ministry by giving him responsibility?' More recently a minister at the end of his first five years of circuit work attended a Further Training course. In the leadership team was a very special person who delighted in all that was positive, and to her the young man responded: 'In one hour you have given me more affirmation than I have had in the last five years.' Just think what that circuit had missed because it neglected the simple human gift of appreciation! Probably the greatest obstacle to developing helpful arrangements for appraisal is the resistance people feel because they think it will be an experience akin to a visit to the dentist. 'What they will do is criticize me!' A good friend, who served me professionally in this matter, gave me a fine model in his own practice. He succeeded in helping me to see my faults and limitations because he took great pains first to give value to good work being done and to recognize abilities being exercised. He helped me to feel good about what I was doing in such a way that I took seriously where I was getting things wrong. Every good teacher knows that a string of negative criticisms will create defensiveness and hinder learning. Appraisal is a form of teaching.

If this is so, the best people to be involved in it are those who themselves have learned and are in process of learning. If you have the responsibility of interviewing people for appointments, you need to have sat in an interviewee's chair. I remember the feeling with which I came out of an interview: 'My, they treated me seriously!' It served to make me sometimes a quite tough but serious interviewer. I tried to honour the seriousness of those who put themselves before us. One has to start with respect. A smile may be an additional bonus but it has no value unless respect is there. This comes from genuine knowledge of what it is like to be in the place of another. When Edward King was Principal of Cuddesdon he was asked to hear the confession of a student. He replied, 'Wait a little. I must make my own first.' And down the road he went to be a penitent before Dr Pusey.[8] We do not want people involved in the appraisal process who are taking an opportunity to exercise power. We want those who accept mutuality in responsibility, who live gratefully, and who are themselves in some way 'under authority'.

For what purposes do we engage in appraisal? It is important for this to be clear to all involved. It is for the development of the Christian community in all its parts. It is to help those who carry particular responsibilities in the community to feel positively towards them. It is to enable expectations to be looked at openly and misunderstandings to be corrected. It is to provide some means of getting a firmer image of oneself in relation to others. It is to identify what actions by different people will contribute to the health of the whole community. It is to enable all involved to see that a good balance is struck between action and the preparation for it. It is to help the whole life of the community to be purposeful.

We know how out of kilter people's expectations of each other can be. Way back in the sixties a group of ministers kept diaries of the time expended on different activities and compared them within the group. As an exercise it had some usefulness, but the results were not revealed to the people who mattered, the people among whom they worked and who had expectations about how ministers should use their time. A church group was once asked to name the activities in which they would like their minister to be involved. Then they were asked to attach an amount of time that should be given to each. At the end it was found that the minister needed to devote more hours to work than there were in any one week. Everyone laughed and they got down to being more realistic in their expectations. In some way (not necessarily that way) this exercise needs to be done. Sometimes it is time that prevents expectations from being realized, but it can be lack of resources, lack of support, lack of energy. To scrutinize an expectation in this way leads the person upon whom the expectation is placed to see that their difficulties are understood and their efforts towards achieving it valued. It may be necessary for the conclusions of such an exercise to be communicated to the congregation more generally, but in some cases it may be sufficient for people simply to know that the issue has been discussed.

It is not good enough for people to have to judge their acceptability on the basis of rude, thoughtless or unkind comments, or of comments by the person who makes most noise. None of us is acceptable to all. It is no real hardship to bear that truth. What we need to know is what our acceptability profile looks like and on what it is based. I have known ministers who have refused an invitation to stay in a circuit for an extended period because a handful of people did not support the invitation. They knew only the view of those few and had no opportunity to listen to the silent majority. If I am doing my job, I expect there to be some opposition. Knowing the fallen nature of humanity, I would find it strange if there was none. Ministers do not need the temperature of warm regard in the congregation to be taken constantly. They do need to know if they are arousing opposition, to what degree and why. Working with others in appraising the life and work of the congregation should enable this to happen. There is of course the danger that, if opposition or lack of acceptability is felt, the minister will adjust his or her action to reduce these things. That itself would be a matter for appraisal! The more positive possibility is that an attempt could be made to take minority views into account and extra attention be given to explanation of what is being done and why. In fact it seems more likely that an un-quantified fear of lack of acceptability will lead to a conformist attitude in the minister and less creative work by the congregation.

By looking at what we have been and are doing it is easier for us to consider what action should be planned and what targets are to be set for the development of our life together. Appraisal that ends simply with a mark given is hardly adequate. There are theological reasons why it should not be adequate. The mission to which the church is called is to bring to reality the promises God gives for our future. Appraisal must have an eschatological dimension; it must ask about what we are seeking to become under the guidance of the Holy Spirit. We shall not be able to realize in a short period all that God is calling us to. We can mark out some of the stepping stones to be reached in our developing pilgrimage. This may involve determining, for example, what educational input is needed into congregational life. What will enable particular areas of growth in discipleship to take place? It may mean that a particular form of service to the community at large should be explored or new kinds of music be available to enrich worship. These things could be given quite precise form and become the basis for satisfying work because their completion would be recognizable.

What happens in every walk of life is that people see the results and not the effort that has to go into achieving them. The people responsible for the effort often feel aggrieved when this is underestimated by those who see only the result. This matters in all tasks undertaken within a community, particularly (though in no way exclusively) when it is based on voluntary service. People should be and need to be thanked. But appraisal needs to reflect in a special way on the balance being given to action and preparation for it. This may mean that sermon listeners need to understand how much time and effort goes into preparation, not only of the particular sermon but into making the preacher the sort of person who preaches good and useful sermons. Sometimes it may mean that some listeners need to tell a preacher that he or she needs to give more care to preparation and more time to reading. It would not seem to me inappropriate if in an appraisal exercise I was asked what I had been reading. I have always held the view that ministers are paid to read and that we short-change our congregations when we fail to replenish our store-cupboard. I ask my colleagues about this and expect to be open to them about how I am getting on in this area.

Appraisal may result in the identification of training needs generally. At one point, when my work was being appraised, it was said: 'When you came into this job one of the things that made us want you for it was that you were quite well-read. The pressures of the last few years have taken the edge off that quality. We think you should go off for a bit, sharpen up again and you will then be more use to us.' I have a friend who gives great attention to appraisal and budgets 5% of his time to developing the knowledge and skills needed for present tasks and for those that are coming over the horizon. Equally it should be the case that, when the development of a congregation as a whole is being appraised, consideration should be given to training needs for officers and most particularly for the ministry of its members in their Christian witness.

Appraisal is important because it helps those involved to see things as a whole, including what things look like from the different perspectives of others. It is important for people of different levels of ability to benefit from it. It will be a pity if appraisal is seen as being for those who tend to perform well in any case. It is there to help limited people to receive affirmation of their qualities and learn how they may put these qualities to good effect. It is often the case that many people of limited ability function poorly because they have not received adequate affirmation in what they do well. Thomas Merton was talking about those well on in their pilgrimage when he described a certain detachment: 'You will be praised, and it will be like burning at the stake. . . You will have gifts, and they will break you with their burden.'[9] For most people praise will lighten their step, and recognition of their gifts will give them proper confidence. Merton knew that most of us who are at an early stage in the quest of holiness need to have 'been praised a little and loved a little'. Appraisal can be the context for this.

I have not here described structures for appraisal. Many congregations are finding that appraisal takes place in a low key, but effective, meeting of ministers and church stewards, or at a circuit level in meetings of the Circuit Leadership Team. Other possibilities are being explored and described. The Birmingham District of the Methodist Church has recently produced a self-appraisal instrument for experimental use, capable of being used also in the context of a group concerned for the development of ministry in the church. In 1984 the Division of Ministries of the Methodist Church published a somewhat rough (I can say that because I was finally responsible for its publication) document to help in this area called *Ministerial Development*. The main features of it were included in my *Making Good Ministers*, published by the Division in 1985. A wide and detailed survey of possibilities is now available in Michael Jacobs' *Holding in Trust*, a book to which those who want to consider these matters more fully should turn.

In the life of ministers and congregations it is important to know what to do with things that cannot be fitted in. At the end of a week there are people you meant to visit who have not been visited. There comes a point when you run out of time to make complete preparation for a sermon: you have to go into the pulpit! There are things you would like to do, and some you promise to do, but you run out of energy. There are tasks a congregation knows it should tackle, but people turn out to be too busy in other ways. When appraisal is finished, we are left with things that cannot be done, and that has to be accepted. There are things we should like to fit in but we know that we may not manage it. What do we do with our failures?

In some cases we can manage with something less than what we hoped to give. At the end of a day or week there may be

people we intended to see but simply had not time. Often I
telephone to say simply what has happened. Sometimes this is
all that is needed; sometimes one can indicate what one hopes
to do. This is generally appreciated as sensible and honest. More
often my frustration has to be turned into prayer and I recognize
that God will be with those for whom I am concerned whether
I am there or not. There is a fussy sort of pastoral care that
wants to do everything and be in on everything. I am not sure
how effective it is. I used to deflate the extravagant enthusiasm
of theological students by telling them that God wants those
who co-operate with him, not those who compete with him.
Fortunately God is everywhere when we are not. When we serve
him rather than compete with him something very important is
being said from which those whom we serve can learn. Something important is also being said when we are happy with our
failures and when the knowledge of them makes us open to
God's continuing grace.

7

Grace and Gratitude

Most of the forces that change and sustain our lives arise from grace and gratitude. I believe this deeply, but it has not been easy to accept. Earlier I made the outrageous suggestion that ministers, perhaps more than most, find it difficult to believe in the gospel. Inevitably my belief arises from my own pilgrimage as well as from my interpretation of what I observe. I must speak in a personal way or keep silence: the most important things are not reported facts or the opinions of others but what Harry Williams called 'beliefs [that have] become part of my own life-blood'.[1]

It is a constant surprise that people react as if it were a new thought when I say that at any one moment I know that I am right. If I did not so believe, I would change my mind and then be right. This is obviously so and applies to everyone! What I also know is that I am only provisionally right, or in the process of becoming right; for I constantly change my mind. It is strange that people do not always agree with me, but I know that is how it is; and they must find it surprising that I do not see things their way. I must listen to them and they to me. This is how we learn. We do not so learn if we pretend that we are not deeply involved in what we believe to be true.

The difficulty of accepting deep down the grace of God certainly affects one's attitude. It may be that everyone else finds no problem here and cheerfully takes to grace with ease. Am I on my own in finding it difficult to receive the good news that I am forgiven, accepted, a loved child of God? I think not, because it is sin that makes for my difficulty and I am not alone in being a sinner.

We sin, as Harvey Cox pointed out,[2] when we refuse to accept the responsibilities we have been given: the seventh Deadly Sin is sloth. Like Adam shuffling off his responsibility on to Eve, we, too, sin against the gift of autonomy. However, St Augustine was right when he so brilliantly expounded the traditional view that the heart of sin is pride.[3] 'The hopeless thing about most really selfish people is that they are so unconscious of their selfishness.'[4] We are so blinded by our selfishness that the blandishments of a Pelagian view of ourselves seem right. We are the masters of our fate. We do not need (at least not entirely) the gifts of God that cannot be achieved or earned. Perhaps we will accept forgiveness, for it is comforting to do so; but if we accept the power of God so that we can do things or gain holiness, we suffer damage to our pride. We should be able to do these things ourselves. So limits are set. If there are not things I have to accomplish myself, what is left of me? So believers filter grace. Some of the gracious work of God is allowed; but there are areas in which we are the constructors, proud of the Towers we build.[5] Vast quantities of energy are needed, singlemindedness is required, and so we become detached from others. People are left at a distance.

My testimony is to a painful journey along which, step by step, I am allowing God to release me from treadmills of many sorts. How wonderful it is to realize and in a strange way feel good about the fact that everybody does not like me! It is odd that I find some difficulty in seeing this, because I have little problem in not liking certain people I know. Why should not the picture others have of me be very different from my own? Can I not only find the truth about myself but like it? Each year I am filled with admiration for those who run the London Marathon. What fine people they are! All that training and preparation, all that good humour. Wouldn't it be wonderful to be one of them next year. Then there is the relief of saying to myself, 'I don't need to be a marathon runner!' It is not that I am lazy but that I do not need that specific thing in order to feel good about myself. When we are making our way in the world we need to make something of ourselves. This is natural and straightforward, but there is the insidious pressure to make ourselves into what others want us to be. The interesting, climactic period of the early thirties is when many people's lives take a new direction. At that point they come to an end of flirting with the hope of popularity and develop the inner freedom to be themselves. Sadly, some miss it. My experience is that this can be a moment when we accept the freedom to step off that particular treadmill. It is the grace of God that gives us leave to do so.

Grace stops any interest in scalp-hunting, whether the scalps are souls won or projects accomplished. I have come to think that public ministry is important but does not matter supremely. It is work with God's very little people that is of lasting importance. I am reasonably sure that on the last day there will be a few people who will point the Judge of all the earth to me and say 'It was he who made the difference'. At the moment this is only known to me and them. It may also be the case that a few others will similarly point and I shall be as surprised as anyone else. It is unnerving, and sometimes very consoling, to go back to a place in which one served and meet people who say 'Do you remember what you said when. . . ?' Of course we don't, but something of us brushed off on them and it made a difference. All these are consolations, by-products of ministry. They do not belong to a treadmill that we trod in the hope of success.

For many years Dr Newton Flew's initial engagement with first-year students at Wesley House, Cambridge was asking the question: 'Is the gospel offer or demand?' In my time for one hour each week for the first term we had to keep going on that question. Sadly, I thought, he had a clear view of what the right answer was and he wanted to win our agreement. That made me resistant to agreeing with him too quickly. There were those who did. 'Creeps,' I thought! My reluctance to agree that the gospel is offer not demand has meant that I have been serious about the question ever since. So Dr Flew's apparent dogmatism turned out to be good teaching. I believe the gospel is fundamentally the offer of God for our redemption. That is at the heart of things; but there are difficulties.

There is a strong theme in the Christian tradition (appearing in many varied places) suggesting that God does make demands upon us in order to prepare us to receive his grace. It is found in Luther's idea of the strange work of Christ (*opus alienum*) by which he exposes our need of him and follows it with the proper work of Christ (*opus proprium*) by which we are redeemed. 'The commandments . . . are intended to teach man to know himself, that through them he may recognize his inability to do good and may despair of his own ability.'[6] So in Luther's experience of a bruised conscience we have the action of God in its demanding form; even a rustling leaf can sound like the wrath of God.[7] When Ignatius Loyola created the *Spiritual Exercises* as an instrument for use in renewing devotion in the Society of Jesus he built the first week around themes intended to expose to the retreatant his independence and uncreatureliness and so weaken confidence in himself and all his concerns. Then in the second to fourth week he could be rebuilt by contemplating and appropriating the work of Jesus in the gospel story. In John Wesley the theme appears in his preaching of the Law in order to prepare his hearers for the gospel Word. However, he made the transition between the demand of the law and the graciousness of the gospel an act of grace by the notion of pre-venient grace, by which, through the Holy Spirit's gift, we are enabled to turn towards God in repentance to receive his further gifts of grace. T. S. Eliot took up the theme in the *Four Quartets* where he speaks of Christ as '. . . the dying nurse'

> Whose constant care is not to please
> But to remind of our, and Adam's curse,
> And that, to be restored, our sickness must grow worse.[8]

I understand this tradition, know its power and want to keep it alive. It has to be seen as marking out one way by which God comes to us. It must not be allowed to diminish the radical quality of grace.

This radical view of grace was much fought over in the early church. We cannot deduce exactly what happened from the limited material available to us in the New Testament. What does seem clear is that there was a considerable difference of view as to how the work of the infant church should develop. It would not be very surprising if the evidence we have is coloured by the views of the writers (in particular Luke and Paul) about the doctrine of grace.

Luke shows how the issue arose among the Greek speaking Christians. When their spokesman, Stephen, was brought before the Jewish Council, the accusation against him was that he had been saying things against the Temple and the Law.[9] In the speech Luke gives him, after a somewhat boring address in which the action of God in Jewish history (well known to his hearers) was described, we have the words in which the dispensability of the Temple is suggested.[10] Among the members of the Synagogue of Freedmen (Greek-speaking Jews) was Saul of Tarsus in Cilicia, and he would have none of it. This was real heresy. On the road to Damascus, however, Saul met the risen Christ:[11] only God could raise from the dead. This experience led him to believe that, if indeed Christ had risen, it was by the sovereign act of God and a new age had dawned. Stephen was right after all. Anything could now happen because all was dependent on what God gave. The prospects were limitless. Even the requirements of Temple worship and obedience to the Law could not set limits. This enabled him to look back upon his struggles, reflect on the conflicts in the world and the general human condition, and see that salvation was possible for all. This could only come through the gracious powers set loose by the radical act of transformation to which the resurrection of Christ was witness.[12] It was not easy for Paul to convince the early church about his radical understanding of grace.

St Paul's view can be summarized in his question (one often repeated by Augustine), 'What do you possess that was not given to you?'[13] It is difficult to live with this penetrating question as long as pride has its place in our hearts. It is not surprising that in the Christian tradition men and women have not been able to sustain a firm view of grace for more than brief periods. The Reformed tradition can be seen in terms of a cycle of attempts to recover radical understandings of grace. Luther saw himself as calling the church back to the Pauline and Augustinian doctrine of grace. He sought freedom from entanglement with salvation by works that grew out of the pride of men and women. He attacked the way this perversion had gained institutional form and stability in a somewhat legalistic penitential system that offered indulgences related to relics and the treasury of merits. Against this huge collusion with human pride and the vested interests of so many, Luther had to set the single but powerful notion that God saves by grace alone. In this he found his own peace and it opened for him a door into a world of freedom.

In our century the Reformed tradition has been renewed against three potential threats from sources of confidence other than grace. Karl Barth saw philosophy, or human reason, as a temptation to find a way around revelation. One cannot receive the truth of God by the activity of the intellect; it can only be given; it is a revelation, an act of God's free, gracious, self-disclosure. When Rudolf Bultmann approached the New Testament, at least one of the factors that affected him was his Lutheranism. If your existence as a Christian could be supported by a sure base in history, it was possible to feel that you rested on firm ground and were not held over the abyss by the powerful uncertainty of faith. Dietrich Bonhoeffer belonged to that tradition too and saw people stabilizing themselves by the practice of religion. He had to say that salvation does not come through religion: it comes only through grace. If one needs to abandon religion in order to find faith, so be it! This is not to say that philosophy, history and religion have no use. The tradition asserts that the faith by which we are saved does not depend on them. We need to pay heed to this tradition.

How difficult it is to attend to the words St John gives us: 'Apart from me you can do nothing.' For Methodists this takes us into a Covenant Service spirituality that has John 15 at its heart. I wonder how deeply the words of the Covenant Service penetrate each year. We are not content that God appoint 'us our place and work' and that 'he himself be our reward'. When matters of where we are to serve come up, we get nervous. There is the frequent discussion about what 'put me to suffering' means. It is obvious in the context of the service that it means

some form of passivity, but that of all things we do not want.
There is a story that Carl Jung prescribed for a patient one
week of doing nothing. When the patient returned he gave an
account of how he had listened to music, read books and so
on. 'But I told you to do nothing,' said Jung. 'Oh, I could not
have done that. I could not have put up with just myself for a
week.' 'No,' said Jung, 'but we have to put up with you.' When
we fill the gap, we fail; but when our passivity is an openness
to God, we are given the experience 'I am yours and you are
mine' and are at peace.

We make our own selfishness, but self-love is a gift of God's
grace. It is the most beautiful of gifts. It gives us a lightness of
step and the capacity to laugh, but the whole idea is met with
suspicion. There are powerful elements in our traditions that
teach us to beware of thinking too highly of ourselves for fear
of pride. Not far away is the thought that self-hatred is required
of us and we may not find it hard to oblige. Augustine, who
taught that the heart of sin is pride, also wrote about self-love.
'He who would give alms . . . should begin with himself.'[14]
'Ourselves we love the more, the more we love God.'[15] We have
to learn to love what God loves, and how hard it is when it
comes to the particular creature that is ourself. When we learn
that we are the objects of God's love, we learn to love ourselves,
not in a self-absorbed way, but delighting in the fact that we
are loved by God.

My experience is that the degree of self-hatred in religious
people is frightening. This is the most characteristic example of
what was called (by Reinhold Niebuhr) 'the persistence of sin
in the life of the redeemed' or the all-too-human in the body of
Christ. I long for such people to hear the wisdom of Jesus Son
of Sirach: 'How can anyone who is hard on himself be kind to
others?'[16] and Bernard of Clairvaux: 'It is laid down that we
should love others as we love ourselves. But were you to love
others as you have hitherto loved yourself, I for one would not
wish to be committed to your care. Learn first to love yourself
and then you can love me'; 'How can anyone be a benefactor
without being also benevolent?'[17] To denigrate oneself is a
recurring characteristic and there is no vaccination that will

prevent further attacks. Once I was dashing to catch a train in London when a colleague called across the road 'Slow down to a gallop!' If he had said 'Walk, don't run', I should have taken no notice. He knew that there must be some reason for haste, but cared enough not to want me to lose something more important by chasing too hard. We shall not destroy the self-deprecation that comes to tie bonds around us at a stroke. We can, however, walk more slowly and open ourselves to grace while seeking the gift of self-love until, with practice, such openness to grace becomes a habit. The sort of death that creeps up on us, when we love ourselves so little, is turned back by the renewing power of God's grace.

I think of a woman who told me how she had spent her life, until her father died, trying to be what she thought he wanted her to be. Comparatively late in life she felt free to be what her heavenly Father created her to be. There are difficulties in translating John 1.4 but I continue to find the NEB version thrilling: 'All that came to be was alive with [the Word's] life.' God's creative act in us is not a mistake. A man in a fellowship group read from the study notes, 'Salvation does not so much make you different as make you whole.' He said, 'Does that mean I do not need to be like those ideal people I have been envying so long, and been constantly disappointed when I don't become like them? Can I become good as me?' That day he found salvation. God forgive us when we try to mould ourselves (and perhaps worse mould other people) into some pre-conceived model of holiness. Thomas Merton wrote: 'A tree gives glory to God first of all by being a tree.'[18] So the best that we have to offer God is what he has made us to be: that and not something different. When we learn this we may not become nicer people. In fact some may find us more gritty and see our angularity uncovered, but there will be authenticity in what we present to the world. In the end that will be what counts.

Much of what I have been saying applies to all Christian disciples. What also concerns all Christians is that their spirituality becomes basically eucharistic. I do not mean that their religious practice must include frequent attendance at holy communion, though that may be the case. It is that their lives as

Christians should be dominated by thanksgiving. In his seminal book on prayer Neville Ward says that eucharist (thanksgiving) establishes 'the nature of the principal Christian act of prayer and also the quality of the essential Christian posture before experience'.[19] 'Thankfulness and appreciation of life unlock the door of the prison of self.'[20] We all know the shrivelling of the person that results from an inability to be grateful. Indeed, we become so used to living with half a heart that we have to re-learn how to be grateful. Margaret Spufford's account of her pilgrimage of suffering is a recent portrait of a eucharistic person.[21]

Jesus frequently offered his disciples the possibility of treating life in an experimental way. In what we now know as the Sermon on the Mount we have a collection of bits of teaching, mostly arranged thematically. In one section[22] he introduces traditional ethical demands with phrases like 'You have heard your forefathers were told' and then follows it up with the suggestion of an alternative behaviour that the disciples might test. For example: 'You have heard that they were told, "An eye for an eye, a tooth for a tooth." But what I tell you is this: Do not resist those who wrong you. If anyone slaps you on the right cheek, turn and offer him the other also.' They knew what happened when they did what retributive justice demanded: there was a brawl. Now what about trying something different? See what it feels like for both parties when you turn the other cheek. Test it for size. Wear this unaccustomed coat, get the feel of it. See whether it might not be a better way. So also: 'Love your neighbour and hate your enemy.' That is surely how it should be. Well, try something else: 'Love your enemies and pray for your persecutors.' See what happens to you and to them when you try this out. What feeling do you have for your persecutors when you start praying for them? I was recently reminded of the preference of Caribbean people for a thank-offering rather than a collection. There is something highly significant in the fact that more is usually received in the former than the latter!

Now we can go back to the Beatitudes[23] and re-read them. Let things turn into blessings and the world is transformed.

Accept what it is to be poor in spirit, and out of this thankfulness find that you inhabit the Kingdom of Heaven. Do not turn away from sorrow as a thing to be rejected; accept it and let it become a blessing, and indeed the gift of consolation will come. It is when we turn towards life with thankfulness, however, difficult it may be at times, that the central structure of our lives is right. Already deaf Beethoven could describe the first movement of his sixth symphony as 'Awakening of feelings of thanksgiving on entering the countryside'. Thankfulness can bring meaning and express the discovery of meaning and significance, even in unlikely things. It was the gratitude for being given a purpose to live for that held Victor Frankl through the horrendous years of his captivity in Auschwitz and Dachau.[24] Those who did not possess such gratitude lost hope and died. When he came to write up his experiences and express what he had learnt in his psychiatric practice, he quoted frequently the words of Nietzsche, 'He who has a why to live can bear with almost any how.' The person who makes fundamental sense of life by gratitude can cope.

What we need more of is celebration at the cost if necessary of less penitence. There was a series of advertisements for cream cakes, including slogans such as 'Naughty but nice' and 'Get this past your conscience'. The message was clear that, if you wanted to be really wicked, you should eat cream cakes. The advertisements struck a chord. Offer a cream cake and people say 'I shouldn't.' Why not? If people are eating half a dozen every day they are probably right to hesitate. Cream cakes, like wine and Christmas pudding, are for celebration. They are not to replace sausage and mash (though that is itself something for celebration) but to add a particular and good dimension to life. It would be foolish to suggest that Christians should go gushing around the world saying thank you. That would be awful. A eucharistic view of life needs moments of celebration, occasions when it justifies every bit of thankfulness we hold in our hearts. I suspect that someone caricaturing me would pepper what I said with 'splendid'. I know it to be one of my favourite words. I may use it boringly, but I would rather that than never use it at all. It is the Amen that runs through my liturgy of thanksgiving. What is important is that it should be addressed not only to those things of which one approves. The affirmation of others has to be thanksgiving for what they are and what they are contributing, even though we may not always like it.

How difficult it is to accept the otherness of people. In 1977 I spent an enriching period teaching in the Andhra Christian Theological College in South India. For the first couple of weeks India was overwhelming and fascinating. In that period I saw the sights of Delhi, travelled to see the Taj Mahal at Agra and then the ordinary and astonishing sights of the twin cities of Hyderabad and Secunderabad, where I was to spend most of my time. It was not long before the heat, the dirt, the crowds, the poverty, insects and reptiles, began to get to me. I remember an awful bus journey when I decided I hated India. But that was the crisis point in the culture fever, and from then I began to recover and love again all that I had delighted in at first and many other things too. So I was irrevocably changed by this love-hate relationship that most who stay longer than a brief visit seem to develop. The critical point is when you recognize how deep the differences are between particular cultures. It is not just that buses are dirtier and more crowded than here, and all the other things. The world is seen in a wholly different way. Later I had to arrange for American seminarians to spend a year working in British Methodist churches. Most of them seemed at first to share the experience of delight in being here, pleasure in the oddness of our accents and in the more obvious signs of a long history around them. There came the point when unexpected culture shock began to be evident. England was not an extension of the United States. They began to see that the Lancastrian was not an American with a funny accent but someone whose mind-set was different from theirs and whose approach to issues was shaped by a different tradition and different values. Then they began really to meet the people with whom they were working, seeing them and honouring them as they were. It seemed to me that this was the richest gift we were able to give our visitors. It was something that would affect their whole lives as ministers. Now they would find it easier to see that people are deeply different from one another, even though they share some degree of common culture. We are fortunate if we are helped to recognize early the fact that other people are not odd but different.

Jung's work on psychological types gives some conceptual basis for our experience of difference. He recognized that people differ fundamentally in the direction of their psychic energy, outwards or inwards; that is, they are extroverts or introverts. He saw that people give different values to intellect, feeling, sensation and intuition. When we recognize the type we are, we begin to see that others are indeed different. It is not that people are just different shades; they are different colours. The introvert sees the world in a radically different way from the extrovert. The question is whether we put up with this fact or enjoy it and are thankful for it. There are then some practical issues to be considered.

Do we really accept variety in vocation with thankfulness? When Christian leaders make somewhat angular statements in the exercise of a prophetic ministry, is our first response to correct the imbalance in their view or to accept it with thankfulness? If the latter, we can go on to see what we can make of it and to find ways of placing it within a total view that would be defective without it. Joshua disliked the ecstatic behaviour of Eldad and Medad and attempted to stop it, but Moses said 'I wish that all the Lord's people were prophets.'[25] This polarization is not helpful. Jesus pointed to a variety of ministries when he instructed the disciples to go out 'like sheep among wolves; be wary as serpents, innocent as doves'.[26] On my first night in Cambridge we (a group of quite cocky young men) were invited by the Principal to sing:

> The gift which he on one bestows,
> We all delight to prove.[27]

I have been trying to respond creatively to that ever since, not without difficulty. It is not easy for some people to take on disturbing ideas. It is not easy for those who have disturbing ideas to keep patience with those whose vocation is to translate the ideas into programmes and structural changes. What makes it easier is a eucharistic slant to all we do.

Some people cannot handle very well the rubbing edges of difference between people. It would be ideal if we could let many flowers bloom and be enriched by their variety. However, not everyone can manage that level of generosity. It may be that we have to accept that in some circumstances it will be right for parallel programmes to exist, enabling like-minded people to enjoy together what is common and familiar to them. If this has to be so, it will still be right to hold before all the duty of gratitude each has towards the other. Within a Christian community some judgment may need to be made as to what degree of difference can be tolerated within it and to what extent the gifts of many contribute to the enrichment of all. Where there are those with strong minority interests, they may feel frustrated, feel that their own needs are not being met and be unable to make a distinctive enough contribution to the whole. In such a situation there is a good case for some parallel activities, styles of worship or spirituality. The same conclusion may be reached if tolerance is low and the chance of polarization is high. In such a case the risk of people being bruised by what is alien to them is high. If, however, the tolerance level is high and people do not make strong demands for the satisfaction of their particular needs, it will be easier for a regime of variety to flourish. What is important is that the respect for other people that arises from gratitude for them should express itself in terms of careful and detailed assessment of what is happening within a congregation.

In any community where there are gladly accepted differences care must be taken in handling conflict and recognizing agreement. Most people do not like conflict, a few revel in it. There are those who are afraid of conflict, and others who feel that differences can be sorted out without the violence implied by conflict. There are those who feel they are likely to win in a fight and use conflict to get their own way. There are those who think that a deep commitment to honesty must go with a preparedness to face up to issues of difference directly. The art of love in a community is to help people make loving responses

to these fears and attitudes. This is not to imply that these
responses will be soft, though sadly this is the general tendency
of Christian communities to their great loss. It is not difficult to
remember times when it was right to help a simmering conflict
between people to come out into the open and be dealt with.
The attachment to a particular view (and its opposite) had been
invested with considerable emotion that needed to be discharged. Here was a test for one's eucharistic orientation
towards people. Could one risk the violence that might come
from heated exchanges, believing that there was, or would be
given, sufficient thankfulness to see everyone through to a
creative solution? It is also easy to remember those times when
there was indeed difference between people, but the best way
forward was a process in which difference would be eroded
step by step as both sides found together a way forward that
could be accepted with gratitude.

Sometimes the problem of a community is to discover what
it agrees about. There can be some current orthodoxy that
people feel is required of them but with which they do not
agree. Individuals may find it difficult to state their view against
the pressure of the orthodoxy that they believe, mistakenly,
is widely shared. Ecumenical discussion can be like this. Co-
operation is a good thing. So, when some suggestion for co-
operation is made, it is not always easy to consider it honestly
or criticize it rigorously, because opposition to it may be seen
as lacking ecumenical commitment. Many discussions about
racism, sexism, sexuality, other faiths, politics, programmes
arising from 'Faith in the City' or 'Mission alongside the Poor',
are hampered in this way. Certain orthodoxies are established
and then views that may be contrary to them, though wide-
spread, cannot be expressed. In such a process people are not
valued in their difference. Pundits want to win at the expense
of those who hold gentler views. It is again an art to feel one's
way into what is happening and then give voice to the non-
orthodox view and offer it a chance to live. It is not to be
regarded as improper manipulation, but rather a high regard
for the hidden opinions of people within a community, when
someone lights a disagreement fuse to see if there is a view

people may find difficult to express. If there is no following for the idea, it will burn out. There is also a time for lighting an agreement fuse to test whether there is unexpressed disagreement. There is a very high chance that the initiative will prompt someone to express a contrary view. This is not a book about the techniques of group and community work. What is important for our purpose is the recognition that it is in matters of this sort that we find expressed a degree of thankfulness for other people in all their variety.

8

Balance and Blessing

There is a univeral tendency towards disaster. Physicists call it the second law of thermodynamics. Others call it 'Sod's' or 'Murphy's law'. It is something like original sin in the system! What we also see happening is a tendency to correct or compensate when things are going wrong. Systems react so that some sort of balance is achieved. It is sometimes called the homoeostatic principle. If I press an inflated balloon, I can feel with my hands that it does not like it; it wants to be what it was. The principle works psychologically. If we receive bad news, we are disturbed and look for ways of explaining things in a way that is less painful. Eventually we may have to face the truth and we do this by a subtle process of adapting to the new situation. This is seen most clearly in the process by which people manage bereavement. In most cases they adjust in time and get their lives in some sort of balance again.

Things tend to work well when an appropriate balance is established. It is no use having a splendid marketing department in a business if you are not producing the goods to sell. Management is keeping the parts of the organization in balance. It is not much use having a well-disciplined school if the staff are not good at teaching. We look for well-balanced people with whom to work. We can find a place for the genius sometimes and we also need the awkward-ideas person. We know, however, that the backbone of any enterprise is provided by those who see things as a whole and their work in a balanced relationship to that of others. Of course, we do not hear so much about these people. It is those who are angular in some way who tend to be noticed. In the nature of things you have to be one-sided in order to achieve major changes. Such people have to carry the cost of taking this position; they live extremely interesting but exhausting lives. Most good people listen to them and say, 'How can I take something of that on board? How can I fit some of that in with all the other things to form a better balance?' Upon these middle-people the quality of an enterprise depends.

It takes a genius so to see things in a new way that nothing is ever the same again. Scholarly opinion may become heavily critical of, say, Freud. It can be pointed out that there are other ways of interpreting what he observed and that many of his conclusions are unsafe. The world, however, looks very different since Freud. We get some distance away from a massive figure like Winston Churchill and are able to recognize more clearly his feet of clay. Nevertheless his towering leadership in a particular period changed the course of modern history. The West should be cautious of feelings of triumph when radical changes occur in eastern Europe. The political constructs based on Marxist ideas can crumble like all political systems, but the ideas set loose in the world by Karl Marx will continue to be important. People of genius are needed to give a spurt to change. The balanced people hold things together and move them on over an extended period.

To have a balanced position does not mean an inevitable commitment to the *status quo*. Balance means that you move ahead and carry the whole enterprise with you. Sometimes this means that careful consideration is given to how much opposition can be tolerated at an early stage in the process of change. Some opposition is simply to change as change. Once people see what the new thing looks like they are prepared to accept it. There may not be a consensus for change, but consent to it. Measuring these things is what we call political skill, a gift that we ought not to distrust but to value.

Ministry in the life of the church may be 'an easier yoke' if certain balances are sought. What are they? Some of them have already emerged and the need for them is well understood. What we have seen as the necessary features of the life of the church and of the Christian disciple have to be held together. It is clear that evangelism and kingdom-issues belong to one another. We know that an effective church needs to have satisfying worship, thoughtful preaching and good pastoral care. What other balances are there that might be cultivated but are not always clearly seen?

St Augustine of Hippo gets into the footnotes of theological books because he was a great creative theologian and his comments on Christian ideas were so encyclopaedic. Nobody who wants to understand the Christian tradition can set him aside. See him in his context and we may recognize a work-a-day pastoral theologian. He did not write his massive book on the *City of God* in order to help mediaeval Popes and Emperors manage Christendom, although it did play that role. He wrote it to help steady a church that was passing through massive changes and approaching new ones. He was giving a perspective on the great human and divine forces at work in the world. When he preached to his congregation on the Psalms or St John it was not to produce commentaries to which others would later turn. Psalms and other scriptures were being read in worship and needed exposition. When he tried to understand and expound the Trinity he was unconcerned with the use that future scholars would make of his speculations. He was writing to help both simple people and the intelligentsia enter into deep places within the Christian tradition they had embraced. This was not all he did. His life was one way and another devoted to pastoral care. The days of scholasticism had not yet come. Theology had not been taken over by academics. Augustine was a working theologian and a thoughtful pastor.[1]

To set Augustine up as a model to be emulated is foolish. Such people do not appear very frequently, and to be given an impossible imitative task is not very helpful. What matters is that ministers in particular should take the idea of balance between theology and pastoral care (or shall we call it thoughtfulness in ministry?) and find ways of expressing it in their own situation. We do not have the Manichees to confound as Augustine did, but there are many other modern problems about creation to be addressed. This is not to engage in an exercise in abstraction. It is to do with how we see the world. We do not have the Donatists to combat but we do have the purists who destroy catholicity by claiming it for themselves alone, and who establish rigid positions that exclude love. There are necessary activities in ministry that must restrict the pastoral theologian role. There is not time for everything, but sufficient time must be given to produce thoughtfulness in ministry. If, for example, people are to be helped to understand the gospel through the eyes of St Paul, remembered facets of his teaching studied in the past will not do. Time must be given to work over the texts afresh, exciting new Pauline studies need to be considered, and what they can mean when translated into the way people live must be pondered. If grounding in a biblical faith is neglected, we fail to offer people the support they need, and the substitute of much activity will not be adequate.

Of all the balances I have failed to achieve I suspect the most important has been between prayer and practice. I think I do not stand alone. The world of the monastery is hidden and rather mysterious to most people, to their great loss. In such places for centuries men and women have been setting out a style of life in which there is a balance between prayer and labour. This cannot be exported just as it is to the lives most Christians now live. It does, however, indicate what are the really important elements in life and their proper balance. It is that which must be reformed in our lives of discipleship.

John Cassian, about the year 415 AD, described a monk pondering his lot. He did not like where he was. He had a poor opinion of his brothers. He found his tasks a burden, and he imagined other and distant monasteries in which life would be far preferable. None of the things that dissatisfied him would be found in the monastery of his dreams.[2] Like an itinerant Methodist minister, he could believe the grass was greener elsewhere and spend his life moving from place to place to find what suited him. What St Benedict did was spoil his chances. He brought stability into monastic life. His *Rule* did not just require a monk to stay where he was and work things out under obedience, it also produced a regime in the monasteries homogeneous enough to minimize fantasies of greener pastures in other places. If you went from one to another you would find them more or less the same!

St Benedict may have drawn from many sources in framing his *Rule*, as St Ignatius of Loyola did in shaping his *Spiritual Exercises*, but what matters is that the results were useful for shaping the lives of the community that had gathered around him. Benedict established the place of prayer by the routine of 'The Hours', the pattern of services running through each day: the reading through of scriptures and not least the psalms being said or sung over each week. In addition were *lectio divina*, the prayerful reading of scripture and other books, and manual labour. The proportion of the elements cannot be applied in a different context, although the monk's six hours of manual work each day is not so different from the time devoted to work by many people today. What we may be tempted to see as the monkish part of the life, the recitation of offices, is nicely balanced with tasks not dissimilar to many undertaken by lay Christians today. What stands firm is the need to balance prayer and practice. It is this that creates stability.

One thing Methodists are not very good at is saying psalms communally. For this to be done well everyone needs to listen very carefully to the others and so achieve something like a single voice. Monastic prayer is not only giving attention to God. It is being attentive to the others in the community so that prayer serves to build up the common life, people joined in prayer and held together. Similarly, the community depends upon each one serving the others in work. 'Let the brethren serve one another';[3] 'They are truly monks when they live by the labour of their hands.'[4] Order, balance and moderation run through the whole life of the monastery. There is no exemption from prayer for anyone, nor from work, except for reason of sickness or infirmity. How we would serve one another more adequately if we gave time to pray for one another! How our attention to the world would be sharpened if we had looked at it in the silence God gives! How our joy in routines might be recovered if we opened ourselves to God's love in the routine of prayer!

In my view one of the less helpful ideas current in the upsurge of interest in spirituality has been the emphasis upon 'being' rather than 'doing'. Perhaps I am missing something, but either I do not understand what is being said or I do not like it. What matters, it is suggested, is the cultivation of the inner life, what one is in oneself. How this can be done apart from the rest of normal human life escapes me. What is more, the idea does not fit well into the main stream of Christian spirituality. St Gregory the Great tends to be known only because he sent St Augustine of Canterbury as a missionary to England. His memory is worth more than this. He was a powerful layman in Rome before becoming a monk. After being called to various duties he became Pope. Gregory's pontificate was one of great achievements. His influence in Italy was enormous. The church had accumulated considerable wealth in land and Gregory put it to good use in a series of charitable projects. He could well have been designated as patron saint for all Mission alongside the Poor. We owe most of our knowledge of St Benedict to Gregory's 'Dialogues'. His commentary on the Book of Job had a lasting influence and centuries later touched both St Thomas Aquinas and Maimonides, the twelfth-century Jewish philosopher. Add his role in establishing the Gregorian chant and we have a record impressive by any standards. This was the man who identified what one is as a part of what one does.

In Gregory's book of *Pastoral Rule* attention is given in Part II to the quality of life of the pastor and in Part III to subjects upon which those in his care should be taught and admonished. Part I is about the inner qualities that drive the pastor. Gregory was concerned chiefly with the bishop in his pastoral role, but what he says can easily be applied more generally. 'There are many . . . who yet desire to teach what they have not learned, who appraise the burden of authority the more highly in proportion to their ignorance of its far-reaching responsibility.'[5] There must be an inner respect for truth and authority before a person can presume to teach or exercise authority. Preachers need to give attention to why they preach and to recognize, for example, whether they are offering service or being driven to it.[6] What matters in all things is to be able to recognize the truth of one's motivation: 'The motive hidden within is one thing, what is taking place on the surface of their conscious mind is another.' Being in a public position is dangerous to the soul: 'A man is quite incapable of learning humility in a position of superiority, if he did not refrain from acting proudly when he was in a position of subjection.'[7] Only those should become pastors 'who now lead a spiritual life. He must have put aside worldly prosperity; he must fear no adversity, desire only what is interior . . . he is quickly moved by a compassionate heart to forgive, yet never so diverted from perfect rectitude as to forgive beyond what is proper.'[8] When Gregory moves on to consider the life of the pastor, what he must teach and for what causes he should admonish others, there is a constant inter-lacing of action and motives. What we are and what we do are so linked that we discover what we are in doing and what we do springs from what we are.

This integration is found in the extraordinary Cistercian monk Thomas Merton. In him we see an unexpected balance between involvement and detachment. It seems artificial to sepa-rate them. He shows us that it is possible to have a style of spirituality attuned to our times. This is no doubt the reason why his writings are so widely read today. In fact he takes us back to the roots of Cistercian spirituality. 'Bernard, like Greg-ory the Great . . . avoided any facile disjunction between con-templation and action.'[9] There are things in Merton we would more or less expect. 'We must get rid of all lesser joys, all false peace, all the loves that are inadequate to satisfy and fulfil the capacities God has given us. Our happiness consists in the recovery of our true nature.'[10] What is less expected is Merton's central emphasis upon the recovery of the true self, given to us in our creation, through the redemptive process by which the false self, created by egocentricity, dies of starvation.[11] This process includes detachment of a special sort. 'The surest asceticism is the bitter insecurity and labour and nonentity of the really poor. To be utterly dependent on other people. To be ignored and despised and forgotten. To know little of respect-ability and comfort . . . I certainly don't mean that in order to be a saint one has to live in a slum, or that a contemplative monastery has to aim at reproducing the kind of life that is lived in tenements. It is not filth and hunger that makes saints, nor even poverty itself, but love of poverty and love of the poor.'[12] So at the end of *The Seven Storey Mountain* Merton says to God 'You have contradicted everything. You have left me in no man's land.'[13] He has been led into solitude, detached from everything so that he can be reminded of his distance from God.

Against all that needs to be set Merton's incredible involvement with his times, his concerns about peace, the Vietnam war, racism and inter-faith questions. It is said jokingly that, when Merton lived in the hermitage in The Abbey of our Lady of Gethsemani, he would go to the main buildings each morning carrying a large case to collect his mail! At that stage in his life, when he appeared most detached, his correspondence was vast and an extended network of friends brought him into deep involvement with the world's affairs. He tells of what sounds like a strangely modern mystical experience. 'In Louisville, at the corner of Fourth and Walnut, in the centre of the shopping district, I was suddenly overwhelmed with the realization that I loved all these people, that they were mine and I theirs, that we could not be alien to one another though we were total strangers. It was like waking from a dream of separateness. The whole illusion of a spearate holy existence is a dream.'[14] To separate being and doing is false. Somehow we have to learn to build into our lives involvement and detachment. This alone is the way to holiness for modern men and women.

I recognize that I have been working with the problems of achieving balance in ministry for many years. Whatever competence has been achieved in some areas, confidence in having got the balance of things right has always been elusive. Perhaps this is a widely shared experience. People seem hesitant to discuss it. It is essential that it should be discussed. We began by considering the tension arising from high ideals and heavy responsibilities. To delineate a problem tends to arouse the expectation that a solution has been found and simply needs to be described. This is not the case. There seems to be no model that can apply in all cases and lead to good management of the problem. Maybe some light has been thrown on features of the problem so that an improved approach can be visualized. We are left with fallible people and Christian communities that are like the curate's egg.

The image of the yoke in this book's title alluded, of course, to the offer of Jesus addressed to all who would be his disciples: 'Take my yoke upon you, and learn from me, for I am gentle and humble-hearted; and you will find rest for your souls. For my yoke is easy to wear, my load is light.'[15] It also has an echo of a 'yoke of slavery',[16] the burden of circumcision and the Law of Moses that should not be a yoke laid on the shoulders of Gentile converts.[17] Not all Christians find the 'yoke of Christ'[18] a burden but too many do. There are some who would respond to such people by inviting them (or telling them!) to pray to God for Christ's offered easy yoke. How can one say they are wrong? Then I remember how helpful my colleague was in saying 'Slow down to a gallop': he was offering something that did not seem an impossible alternative. So I have suggested the possibility of 'an easier yoke' and attempted to point to some ways in which it could be realized. The fact remains that wearing a yoke implies that there is a load to be pulled or carried. There will be a burden if the load and the strength to bear it are mismatched. It is no use praying for relief when there is an alternative and when what needs to be done is quite clear. There must be off-loading. Sensible objectives must be set; work must be properly distributed, and so on. There may be some basic silliness in people's approach to the task that must be dealt with. There may be much energy being used unproductively on inner conflicts, energy that needs to be transferred to the significant job.

We have learned that there are other things that matter. A yoke can be a cross-piece enabling horses or oxen to draw a load; it can be timber shaped to fit a person's shoulders so that two pails can be carried. It is this second meaning that indicates how important balance is. Keeping two things in balance is one thing, but when the number of responsibilities increases beyond a handful the stress experienced is due not simply to accumulated weight but to divided responsibility. It is when I have to keep too many balls in the air at the same time that disaster is near. Handling the competing claims of too many things is a balancing act that takes up energy in addition to the tasks themselves. Finding ways of balancing things comfortably – wearing an easier yoke – is worth investing some time in. The balances we have referred to in this chapter could be seen as additional burdens tending to increase the stress. I think they are not. Theological thoughtfulness removes some of the less important tasks from our agenda and makes the purpose of others so much clearer that their weight appears to be relieved. Prayer balancing action releases power for action. Making sure that being and doing, motivation and performance, detachment and involvement, are one thing, not added activities yields a surplus rather than a deficit in an audit of resources. I hope there have been sufficient pointers for readers to recognize where the balances need to be struck in their own different and special circumstances.

In a symposium on Holy Communion,[19] Gordon Rupp referred rather naughtily to the prayer of Humble Access in the communion service of *The Book of Common Prayer* as 'Cranmer's trip wire'. The service had begun with the collect for purity and continued with the prayer for mercy in response to the recitation of the ten commandments, then after the Exhortation there had been a further call to penitence and to prayer for forgiveness, with the Comfortable Words giving assurance of God's acceptance of penitent sinners. Before communion, however, Cranmer introduced the prayer that got the congregation down on its knees again, in case somehow it had not caught the point earlier.

Just in case I have not been heard, let me indicate for the last time the fundamental perspective of this book: Christian ministry is a blessing not a burden! Blessings come from God. We may bless one another on God's behalf but we do not bless ourselves: that is a gift to be received. When Jesus spoke of the 'blessed', those who had received the blessing of God, he did not make the blessing directly conditional upon any action of theirs. Blessedness comes as a by-product of seeking something else. When people are poor in spirit, sorrowful, gentle, hungry for righteousness, merciful, pure, peacemakers, victims in the cause of right, then they are open to receive God's blessing. It can never be commanded, only prayed for.

When we have responded with good sense to our situation, when we have stopped deceiving ourselves or others, when we have done the necessary work, we may be in a position to put God's gift to good use. At that time we shall pray for an easier yoke, and God will answer our prayer and make the way of our discipleship a blessing. We may even have the courage to seek an easy yoke, but I suspect that such seeking may be either so presumptuous that we shall never be trusted to carry our easier yoke, or such a pure act that we shall not need it in any case.

When the barbarian invasions were sweeping over north Africa in the fifth century, Bishop Honoratus asked St Augustine what Christian ministers should do. Should they stay at their posts or flee to help the refugee Christians? In his reply[20] the issues were carefully discussed, but at the end Augustine expressed his hope that bishops and priests would stay when the going was hard 'glowing with love and satisfying the claims of love'.

Lord, you have taught us that all our doings without love are nothing worth. Send your Holy Spirit and pour into our hearts that most excellent gift of love, the true bond of peace and all virtues, without which whoever lives is counted dead before you. Grant this for the sake of your only Son, Jesus Christ our Lord.

Collect for the Seventh Sunday after Pentecost

Notes

1 Pressures and Purposes

1. I Cor. 1.26.
2. Luke 12.35–40.
3. Acts 1.8.
4. R. W. Raven (ed.), *The Dying Patient*, Pitman 1975, p. 93.
5. Matt. 8.20.
6. F. Baker (ed.), *Letters of John Wesley*, Oxford University Press 1980, Vol. I, p. 223.
7. Also *General Rules of Employing Time* (nine of them) and *General Rules of Intention*; see Henry D. Rack, *Reasonable Enthusiast*, Epworth Press 1989, p. 82. Later there came 'Rules of The Society' 1743 and 'The Twelve Rules of a Helper' 1753, now bound into volume I of *The Constitutional Practice of the Methodist Church*, Methodist Publishing House 1988.
8. Quoted by Gordon Rupp, *Religion in England 1688 – 1791*, Oxford University Press 1986, p. 394.
9. H. Lindstrom, *Wesley and Sanctification*, Epworth Press 1946, p. 158.
10. No. 148, *Hymns and Psalms*, Methodist Publishing House 1983.
11. e.g. Dr Hugh Eadie's studies of the Church of Scotland, *Contact*, Summer 1975.
12. *Church Times*, 29 December 1989.
13. Anders Nygren, *Agape and Eros*, SPCK 1953, p.78.
14. Jürgen Moltmann, *Theology of Hope*, SCM Press 1967, p. 21.
15. Esther de Waal, *Seeking God*, Collins 1984, p. 153.

2 Necessities and Non-essentials

1. *The Ascent of Mount Carmel* ii. 7; E. A. Peers (tr. & ed.), *Complete Works of St John of the Cross*, Burns & Oates 1935, Vol. I, pp. 85–86.

2. Roy Campbell (tr.), *St John of the Cross: Poems*, Penguin 1960, p. 35.
3. *The Interior Castle* VII. iv; K. Kavanaugh & O. Rodriguez (trs), *Teresa of Avila: The Interior Castle*, SPCK 1979, p. 192.
4. Luke 10.38–42.
5. Acts 10.36.
6. Eph. 4.11.
7. George G. Hunter, *To Spread the Power*, Abingdon Press 1987, pp. 100f.
8. Cf. Roger Fisher & William Udy, *Getting to Yes*, Hutchinson 1982.

3   *Diversity and Direction*
1. Thomas Merton, *Bread in the Wilderness*, Burns & Oates 1954, pp. 55–56.
2. Robert Browning, *Fra Lippo Lippi*.
3. Elizabeth Barrett Browning, *Aurora Leigh*, Bk vii.
4. T. S. Eliot, *East Coker* V in *Four Quartets*, Faber 1944.
5. Ex. 33.29.
6. John 14.2.
7. Matt. 28.5.
8. Matt. 28.10.
9. Mark 16.6.
10. Luke 24.13–32.
11. John 20.20–26.
12. T. G. Tappert (ed.), *Luther: Letters of Spiritual Counsel*, SCM Press 1955, p. 34.
13. Peter Baelz, *The Forgotten Dream*, Mowbrays 1975.
14. *The Constitutional Practice and Discipline of the Methodist Church*, Vol. 2, Section 2 (4), p. 212.
15. A report to the 1988 Methodist Conference.
16. I Kings 3.9.
17. 1974 Methodist Conference statement *Ordination*, paragraph 14.
18. *Ordination*, paragraph 16.

4   *Comprehensiveness and Containment*
1. Augustine speculated in this way about *rationes seminales* being the source of an evolving creation.
2. Cf. Stephen W. Hawking, *A Brief History of Time*, Bantam Press 1988.
3. No. 109, *Hymns and Psalms*, Methodist Publishing House 1983.

4. Sermon 184; Q. Howe Jr. (tr. & ed.), *Selected Sermons of St. Augustine*, Gollancz 1967, p. 47.
5. John 1.2.
6. Col. 1.16.
7. John 4.14.
8. II Cor. 6.5.
9. Matt. 28.19.
10. Report of the Department of Christian Citizenship to the Methodist Conference.
11. Dom Gregory Dix, *The Shape of the Liturgy*, Dacre Press 1945, p. 744.
12. Philip Luscombe, 'Churches and Congregations', *Epworth Review*, January 1991, pp. 59–67.
13. The sociological concept used in the WCC study might now be replaced by a 'systems' model, with which many are now familiar and which links with St Paul's view of the church as the Body of Christ.
14. John 21.25.
15. *On the Trinity* VI. x. 11; Augustine, *The Trinity*, Fathers of the Church Vol. 45, The Catholic University of America Press 1963, p. 213.
16. Col. 1.15.
17. For this understanding I have long been in debt to John Tinsley; see his *Tell it Slant*, Wyndham Hall Press, Indiana 1990.

5 *Motives and Morale*
1. A. H. Maslow, *Motivation and Personality*, Harper & Brothers 1954.
2. J. Telford (ed.), *Wesley's Veterans*, Wesleyan Conference Office 1914, Vol. V, p. 132.
3. Luke 14.28–33.
4. I Tim. 3.2.
5. Ps. 30.5.
6. On this see the fine exposition by Teilhard de Chardin in a chapter 'The Divinisation of our Passivities' in *Le Milieu Divin*, Collins 1960.
7. In M. H. A. Melinsky (ed.), *Religion and Medicine*, SCM Press 1970, pp. 93f.
8. I have seen the same thing happen with students on practical placements during training for Christian ministry.
9. Ecclus. 10.2–3.
10. Douglas McGregor, *The Human Side of Enterprise*, McGraw-Hill 1960.

11. By J. F. Morris; see Ralph Ruddock, *Roles and Relationships*, Routledge & Kegan Paul 1969, p. 49.

6   *Accountability and Appraisal*
1. *The Expository Times*, May 1970.
2. See, e.g., Carl Rogers, *Client-Centred Therapy*, Houghton Mifflin 1951.
3. This view was supported in an influential book by R. R. Carkhuff, *Helping and Human Relations*, Vol. I, Holt, Rinehart & Winston 1969, in which he emphasized confrontation as one of the facilitative conditions of effective therapy.
4. Matt. 18.15–17.
5. S.O.425 (3), *The Constitutional Practice and Discipline of the Methodist Church*, Vol. 2, Methodist Publishing House 1990.
6. Under S.O.111 (2), ibid.
7. Cf. Michael Jacobs, *Holding in Trust*, SPCK 1989, pp. 19f.
8. John A. Newton, *Search for a Saint*, Epworth Press 1977, p. 45.
9. Thomas Merton, *The Seven Storey Mountain*, Sheldon Press 1975, p. 422.

7   *Grace and Gratitude*
1. H. A. Williams, *The True Wilderness*, Constable 1965, p. 8.
2. Harvey Cox, *On Not Leaving It To The Snake*, SCM Press 1968.
3. It was claimed by A. Nygren (*Agape and Eros*, SPCK 1953, p. 485, followed by E. G. Rupp, *The Righteousness of God*, Hodder & Stoughton 1953, p. 165) that Augustine's view was that man is curved towards the earth, pulled down by the weight of earthly things; whereas for Luther man is curved in on himself, corrupted essentially by his dominating self-concern. Though Augustine uses the word *curvatus* in relation to earthly desires, it is wholly wrong to suppose that he does not in any way see sin as egoism. Nobody knew more deeply than Augustine the centripetal force that directs us all.
4. R. N. Flew, *The Forgiveness of Sins*, Epworth Press n.d., p. 14.
5. Gen. 11.4.
6. Luther, *The Freedom of the Christian Man*, H. J. Grimm (ed.) *Luther's Works*, Vol. 31, Fortress Press 1957, p. 348.
7. See E. G. Rupp, *The Righteousness of God*, pp. 108–9.
8. T. S. Eliot, *East Coker* IV in *Four Quartets*, Faber 1944.
9. Acts 6.13.
10. Acts 7.48–50.
11. Acts 9.5 and very importantly I Cor. 15.8.

12. It is not my purpose here to give the detailed exposition of St Paul to justify this view. For me these ideas have come to fresh life in books such as E. P. Sanders, *Paul and Palestinian Judaism*, SCM Press 1977, and John Ziesler, *Pauline Christianity*, Oxford University Press 1983.

13. I Cor. 4.7.

14. *Enchiridion* XX.76 in *Augustine: Confessions and Enchiridion*, tr. Albert C. Outler, Library of Christian Classics Vol. VII, SCM Press 1955, p. 384.

15. *The Trinity* viii. 12 *in Augustine: Later Works* tr. John Barnaby, Library of Christian Classics Vol. VIII, SCM Press 1955, p. 53.

16. Ecclus. 14.5.

17. Letter 9 in B. S. James (tr. & ed.), *The Letters of Saint Bernard of Clairvaux*, Burns & Oates 1953, p. 39 and Letter 223, ibid., p. 303.

18. Thomas Merton, *(New) Seeds of Contemplation*, Anthony Clarke Books 1962, p. 23.

19. J. Neville Ward, *The Use of Praying*, Epworth Press 1967, p. 20.

20. Ibid., p. 24.

21. Margaret Spufford, *Celebration*, Collins 1989.

22. Matt. 5.21–48.

23. Matt. 5.3–10.

24. ˙ ˙.ctor Frankl, *Man's Search for Meaning*, Hodder & Stoughton 1964.

25. Num. 11.28–9.

26. Matt. 10.16.

27. No. 753, *Hymns and Psalms*, Methodist Publishing House 1983.

8 Balance and Blessing

1. I argued for such a view in my *St Augustine: Pastoral Theologian*, Epworth Press 1974; see also F. Van Der Meer, *Augustine the Bishop*, Sheed & Ward 1961.

2. *Institutes* X.ii in E. C. S. Gibson (tr.), *John Cassian: Institutes and Conferences*, Nicene & Post-Nicene Fathers, 2nd Series, Vol. XI, James Parker & Co. 1894.

3. Rule xxxv in J. McCann (ed. and tr.), *The Rule of St Benedict*, Burnes and Oates 1952, p. 87.

4. Rule xlviii; ibid., p. 111.

5. I. preface in H. Davis (ed.), *St Gregory the Great, Pastoral Care*, Ancient Christian Writers Vol. XI, Longman, Green and Co. 1950, p. 21.

6. I.vii; ibid., pp. 32–34.

7. I.ix; ibid., pp. 36–37.

8. I.x; ibid., p. 38.

9. Rowan Williams, 'Bernard of Clairvaux' in Gordon S. Wakefield (ed.), *A Dictionary of Christian Spirituality*, SCM Press 1983, pp. 44f.

10. T. P. McDonnell (ed.), *A Thomas Merton Reader*, Lamp Press 1980, p. 313.

11. Monica Furlong, *Merton*, Collins 1980, pp. 149f.

12. Thomas Merton, *(New) Seeds of Contemplation*, Anthony Clarke Books 1962, pp. 194–5.

13. Thomas Merton, *The Seven Storey Mountain*, Sheldon Press 1975, p. 420.

14. *Conjectures of a Guilty Bystander* (1966), quoted in *A Thomas Merton Reader*, Lamp Press 1980, p. 345.

15. Matt. 11.29–30.

16. Gal. 5.1; I Tim. 6.1.

17. Acts 15.10.

18. The Covenant Service, *The Methodist Service Book*, Methodist Publishing House 1975.

19. H. Martin (ed.), *Holy Communion*, SCM Press 1947.

20. Letter 228 in J. G. Cunningham (tr.), *Letters of St Augustine*, T. & T. Clark 1875, Vol. II, pp. 425f.